Thanking
Our Soldiers

Thanking Our Soldiers

Random Acts of Gratitude and Generosity Toward Members of the Military

Compiled from Listener Submissions to
America's Morning Show with Quinn and Rose

Rose Somma Tennent

With a Foreword by
Sean Hannity

and an Interview with
Charlie Daniels

Author's/Publisher's Note: The text and letters contained in this volume are used with the express written permission of each contributor.

Cover photograph: © Jason Swarr
Cover and book design by Bill Bingham

Copyright © 2012 by David Productions

ISBN 978-0-7414-8011-8

Published and produced by:
DAVID PRODUCTIONS, INC.
store@warroom.com

Printed in the United States of America

Published November 2012

INFINITY PUBLISHING

Toll-free (877) BUY BOOK
Local Phone (610) 941-9999
Fax (610) 941-9959
Info@buybooksontheweb.com
www.buybooksontheweb.com

Contents

Foreword
Sean Hannity

When my friend and media colleague Rose
Tennent—co-host of the syndicated *America's Morning Show with Quinn and Rose*—asked me to write
the foreword to a book she was compiling on good
deeds done for our soldiers, I was anxious to read
the letters Rose received from her listeners. My personal experience over the years in support of our
troops and veterans has been an ongoing source of
satisfaction to me, as well as to all those involved in
such events as the annual Freedom Concerts. It has
been an honor for me to play a small part in helping
to raise funds for our military families, who deserve
our thanks and the continuing respect of all Americans for their selflessness and service.

And that's what this book is all about—expressing thanks to those soldiers. Rose's radio show,
which has its flagship station in Pittsburgh, was the
vehicle for requesting stories about incidents of gratitude and generosity to the troops. Over a period of
several years, Rose received hundreds of letters
from her listeners, from all over the country, that described small, simple, and heart-warming incidents
in which ordinary citizens did something wonderful
for members of the military. People saw someone in
uniform in a diner, and they paid his or her check.
Grateful citizens walked up to soldiers and thanked

them for their sacrifices. Businesspeople heard about the needs of a military family and refused to accept payment for work done. Scouts and others sent packages to overseas troops. Airline passengers or attendants reported warm receptions given military men and women on flights home.

Despite common themes, each story is told in the writer's own words and the incidents show a wide variety of circumstances. I was happy to find that in this book there are not only letters from average people who talk about their good deeds, but from the military members themselves, and also from their families, who express how grateful they are for those gestures of thanks. Listed in the last chapter is information about dozens of organizations that readers of this book can contact to continue the process of giving back to our troops and veterans.

You can't read through these inspirational stories without getting choked up. In fact, countless letter-writers express how these deeds caused the participants to well up with tears of joy. I suspect you will experience that same reaction when you read the interview with country music legend Charlie Daniels, whose boldly expressed patriotism is contagious.

The thread that runs through all of this is one of basic American goodwill—the spirit of giving and gratitude that often marks the characters of those for whom patriotism is a way of life.

We can absolutely say to all of the people whose stories are in this book—who gave or received, who served with honor or honored someone's service—"You're a great American."

Introduction
How Ordinary Americans Show Their Gratitude to Those Who Serve

Rose Somma Tennent

For the past several years, I have been using the airwaves to encourage support for our troops. I tapped into our very generous audience through the nationally syndicated radio program that I co-host, *America's Morning Show with Quinn and Rose.*

It all started one morning as I related my own story on the radio. I was dining outdoors at my favorite local restaurant. From where I was sitting I could barely see inside a doorway to a private dining room. But what I could see was a few servicemen in uniform being led into that room. I thought it would be a nice gesture to ask their waitress for their bill. When she came outside to my table I told her I wanted to anonymously pay for their lunch.

Now, remember, I saw about four or five guys go in and I figured it would be a decent-sized tab—but I was feeling generous, so why not? The waitress must have been concerned about the size of the tab, since she kept asking me about paying the bill. I said I was paying it, and she agreed to let the guys know that someone who appreciated their service was treating them to lunch. When she brought me the check, it was suddenly clear to me why she had asked me so many times if I really wanted to do this. It turned out those four or five guys had joined about fifteen others who were already seated prior to my arrival!

To this day, when I visit that restaurant we still laugh about how surprised I was when presented with the check. While it was a surprise, I was very happy for the opportunity.

After sharing that story with my audience, I realized I had a unique chance to promote something very dear to my heart—acts and messages of gratitude for our military men and women to thank them for their great sacrifices. Through our weekday morning broadcasts and our website (www.warroom.com), I was able to encourage our wonderful listeners to get involved. E-mails and photos poured in with simple but heartwarming tales. The results of using my radio platform produced a steady stream of tales of giving back, which continues to this day unabated.

This book is the result of several years of collecting amazing "support-the-troops" stories. Many of the original contributors have asked to see these stories compiled in a form accessible to a nationwide reading audience. All of them have given their enthusiastic consent to have their letters included in this book. My listeners and I have all agreed that there is a vital need for something like this. Even as public opinion ebbs and flows regarding the deployment of our troops in all parts of the world, we must never forget the debt we owe the men and women who protect us. These men and women unselfishly serve their country and are willing to spend time away from those they love in order to do so.

This book provides a great variety of acts of Kindness toward our military members, yet many are similar to my story above. These unique and personal stories come directly from the letters sent to the show. Each tells of an opportunity seized by quick-thinking, generous, and patriotic Americans. I have no doubt you will agree with me that these stories are profoundly touching. It seems that the givers were moved at times by their own acts of kindness every bit as much as the receivers.

For those who have perished in war—and those who remain in the battle—thank you. Thank you for loving our country, for helping secure our freedoms, and for ensuring our children's future. Thank you for the blood that was spent on the preservation of those things we hold dear.

The noted historian Henry Armitt Brown said of the Battle of Valley Forge, "They ... fought not for conquest, not for power, not for glory, not for their country alone, not for themselves alone. They served for posterity; they suffered for the human race; they bore here the cross of all the peoples; they died here that freedom might be the heritage of all. It was humanity which they defended; it was liberty herself that they had in keeping."

Brown's words apply to us today every bit as much as they did when they were first spoken. How can we possibly begin to match in our gratitude what they offer daily in their service?

At times it may seem as though no act of generosity toward them could ever be enough. Yet, as shown in this book, our simple acts are received with great warmth and appreciation. Many of us don't know where or how to begin to say thank you. I believe this book gives us a place and a way to begin.

Thanking Our Soldiers opens with an inspiring, patriotic interview with country-music legend Charlie Daniels and ends with a list of organizations and websites that can be contacted by those who wish to pursue similar acts of support for our troops. Finally, I wish to thank my good friend Sean Hannity, talk-radio superstar and noted supporter of our military, for graciously agreeing to compose the foreword to this tribute to our military and the citizens who love and support them.

God bless our troops!

1
An Interview with Charlie Daniels

Rose conducted this 2010 interview with legendary musician Charlie Daniels, a patriotic supporter of our military, for broadcast on America's Morning Show with Quinn and Rose.

ROSE: I had the honor to be at Charlie Daniels's concert in the Pittsburgh area just a few weeks ago. Because I believe he is such a patriot, I asked him to join us today. As you all know, we do a weekly segment on this show entitled "Thanking a Soldier." Charlie, thanks very much for joining us.

CHARLIE: It's an honor to be with you. Thanks for having me on.

ROSE: We do this segment about thanking our soldiers. I ask our audience to send me their stories because I found that it encourages other people to do the same and offers ideas on how to creatively thank someone who is serving our country. I thought that you might appreciate this and that you might have some ideas for others as well. Especially when we have so many hot news topics and so many other things going on, we tend to forget that we still have men and women who are serving overseas right now.

CHARLIE: I will never forget. Every day I pray for these people. I am older than many folks right now—I go back to the Second World War. I remember the day Pearl Harbor was bombed. I remember growing up in a country where patriotism was everywhere. Patriotic songs, all those radio shows where we sat around and listened together: they all were all pro-military—all the magazines, all the newspapers, all the people. Everyone was involved in the war effort.

You know, my brand of patriotism came from those days during World War II when you really had to imagine what was going on. We didn't have TV, just a still picture or a newsreel once in a while. I recall one day in Georgia my mom getting me up early to go to church. The building was jammed with people—everyone was there to pray for the troops because it was D-Day. That's the kind of country that I came from and the kind of place that I still live in when it comes to our servicemen. We owe them an unpayable debt of gratitude. The least we can do is remember them every day of our lives and remember where they are and what they are doing. Our attitude and our caring is the most important.

I have been among these people in three desolate spots in the last few years. The main thing beyond the entertainment—Lord knows they need a distraction—is the fact that somebody cared enough to come. They are comforted in knowing that there are people in this country who care about and appreciate what they are doing. If you know somebody in the service, mail means so much—e-mails, phone calls—when they are at some base in Iraq or some desolate spot in Afghanistan, or wherever they happen to be stationed.

ROSE: And their families that are still here—if we know of a military family in a neighborhood, we should really be looking after them. That should be our top priority.

CHARLIE: Look after their families, supply their needs. Our troops are up against it every day. I was in Iraq in spring and the weather was hot, 120 degrees, and these guys were in full battle dress with full body armor. Put on about thirty pounds of stuff and walk into a sauna and stay all day long, and you get some idea of what they are going through on a day-in-day-out basis and how much dedication it takes for somebody to do that. And they do it with a smile, they do it with conviction, because they know why they are there. These men and women have a clear-cut idea of what their mission is—more so than many of the politicians in this country.

ROSE: You know, it is fascinating to me that we continue to produce young men and women who care that much for their country. This is a volunteer service—no one has forced them to go overseas, and yet they are there. Many times you hear stories about these young men and women who want to return as soon as they come home for a leave—they want to go right back.

CHARLIE: I have been to the field hospitals and to the hospitals in Washington, and have seen people who have been really messed up in the war. And they always say, "I have to get back to my unit." And it's a unit, it's brothers and sisters—people who really care about each other. When they say no man left behind, that's for real. These guys never leave anyone behind. Each unit is a bonded bunch of brothers and sisters, where everyone watches the other guy's back. The finest Americans that exist are the ones you see in uniform. If the caliber and discipline of the youth in this country were half of what they are with the men and women in the military, this would be a totally different land. They're drug-free, they're healthy and bright-eyed, and they have a great sense of mission and self-responsibility. They're the best we've got—they truly are.

ROSE: They *truly a*re. And one of the things that I'd like to get across to people is that no matter how you personally feel about this war or about past wars, these are still young men and women with conviction, and they are over there sacrificing so much in so many ways. I wanted to encourage people to do something for them and for their families—perhaps when they see someone in uniform in a restaurant, pick up a check. I've gotten so many creative ideas on how people thank soldiers. One woman who works in a bakery said that whenever a soldier or family member comes in to pick up a cake, she won't charge them—she won't even tell them. When they come to pick it up it's already paid for.

CHARLIE: Absolutely. And the main thing is that the soldiers know that people care and appreciate what they are doing. Any way you can show that—any small way—is meaningful: whether by writing a letter, picking up a lunch tab, or seeing someone in an airport with desert boots on and saying, "Welcome home!" You know, it's the attitude that counts, as much as the magnitude of what we do.

They take a chance every day, but it's not easy for them. We think maybe, well, they're callous. There was this guy who came into our tent in Baghdad. The guy looked liked Rambo on steroids—he had the shaved head, he had muscles like you wouldn't believe, he was in combat gear—he was the person that you would like to think was standing between you and the enemy. This guy came in and broke down and cried. I've seen that happen with people just like him, people you never would think would react that way. They care. They miss their families just as much as you would miss yours if you were away from them for a year. They worry about their children; they worry about the welfare of their families, how they are doing, if they have enough to get by on, and what kind of neighborhood they're living in. Everything that you worry about if you are a spouse or parent—they have the same worries, except they are four thousand or so miles away. And the only way they can keep in touch is by telephone or snail mail or if they are lucky enough to have e-mail access.

Don't believe they ever get to the point where they shut everything out. They do not shut anything out. They carry pictures of their children, and they will show them to you very quickly—"This is my little girl," "This is my family." They miss their families as much as anyone.

If I ever saw anybody spit on a serviceman, as old as I am, I probably would have to walk up and slug that person. I have heard some politicians say negative things about the military and it makes me so angry. Here you have some pompous politician sitting in a safe office in Washington, D.C., with security and all the benefits, insurance, and retirement plans, and that guy is denigrating men and women who are serving in 120-degree weather in some dusty hell hole, taking their lives in their hands every day—and it makes me just livid. So, you know, if you can't respect the people who protect our freedom and who stand in the gap between us and the enemy, you are a pretty sorry human being in my eyes, and I don't care how far you go in politics.

ROSE: I agree with you, and you make some excellent points and present some things to consider that I haven't even thought of. Especially about those day-to-day things that we all struggle with—of course our servicemen and servicewomen do also, so I want to thank you for that reminder. Charlie, you have always possessed a great sense of patriotism, which shows up powerfully in your recent album release, *The Land That I Love.* Can you talk about why your patriotism and love for this country has always been, and continues to be, so strong?

CHARLIE: I have not been everywhere in the world but I've been to quite a few places on this globe, and I promise you there is no place on Earth like the United States of America. We have problems here; I understand that. We have bad politicians in certain places, we have greedy people, we have unconscionable people. But to get right down to the bottom of it, I will just give you an example. We had what they call a thousand-year flood in Nashville, Tennessee, recently. The water had never been that high, people were stranded, old folks stuck in their homes in neighborhoods that had never been flooded before. The water was coming into the houses. *And nobody waited on the government—nobody waited for anything.* People got into their boats and went around their neighborhoods and rescued their neighbors—old people who had to be carried out with their oxygen tanks. Some folks set up food stands at their own expense to serve others. Some took people they didn't even know into their homes and gave them a place to stay. There were so many donations of household items that they had to turn some down. I am not bragging on my part of the world—although I do brag occasionally since it is a wonderful part of the world—but what I am saying is that feeling for your neighbor is a form of patriotism. When something catastrophic happens, if another fellow human being is in danger, it brings out the patriotism in people; sometimes it's hidden down low, but it's there, in almost every American.

So if you are listening to me and you are a young person wondering about this country: Yes, we have problems, but our problems are magnified a hundred times in so many other countries. You're free in this country. That freedom is worth fighting for, worth voting for, worth standing up for. That is patriotism—caring about not just your country now but what it's going to be like ten years from now. It is also caring about history—the true history of this country, with George Washington, Abraham Lincoln, Paul Revere, and other authentic American heroes— so that it is remembered and taught to your children. Then they will know what a great country we came from and still live in, and that we care about leaving an even better country for them and all our grand-children. That's called patriotism.

ROSE: I have watched you over the years and have seen your involvement, your commitment to the country and our troops. I just want to say thank you on behalf of our listeners, and God bless you.

CHARLIE: Well, thanks—my pleasure. It's been a real honor.

2

The Kindness of Strangers

While we were living in southern Texas, my reservist neighbor was called up. Our properties were a full acre, mainly grass that needed to be mowed once a week for ten months a year, much of it in 100-degree weather. With three small children and a full-time teaching job, it would be a real chore for his wife to mow the grass, so I mowed their property until he returned. I once heard a military wife comment on the radio: "I appreciate the ribbons—I just wish someone would watch my children so I could get a haircut." Perhaps those who can't afford to pay for a meal can afford some time for a military wife or family.

William
Pittsburgh, Pa.

Merry Christmas! I just gave myself an early present.
I was getting my lunch to go at a local Chinese

restaurant and noticed a table of seven Marines. On the way out I asked the man at the register if someone had picked up the tab for the Marines yet. (I almost hoped they had, because then I would be off the hook.) I went ahead and paid the bill, and then left without a word. Man, do I feel good.

Patrick
Wooster, Ohio

Greetings, again! I have had my second chance to bless a soldier.

My family was at a restaurant in Ohio when we noticed a party in the corner. A young soldier, his wife, and their baby daughter were having dinner with their friends.

We had a gift card for our meal, but after my wife and I exchanged knowing glances, I gave it to the young man on his way out, thanking him for his service. He thanked me and went on his way. Our kids asked why we did that, and they learned a lesson about gratitude.

God bless you and Jim and the work you do, and God bless our men and women in uniform.

Patrick

I'm an airline flight attendant and about a week ago I worked a flight from Charlotte, North Carolina, to San Francisco. We had a soldier dressed in fatigues on the flight who had just come back from Iraq. He was on his way home to meet his friends and family. He was sitting in the back of an Airbus 321 (a big plane). The crew definitely took care of him throughout the flight. Toward the end of the flight, he came to the back galley and said he was so excited about coming home and seeing his family that his heart was about to burst.

On landing, a flight attendant announced that this soldier was returning from Iraq and thanked him for his service. He also asked the passengers to please stay seated and let him get off first to meet his family. When we pulled up to the gate (much to my surprise), no one moved. The soldier took a few moments to get his carry-on bags out of the overhead bins and still nobody moved—not even the first-class passengers! As he walked up the aisle, he was given an ovation by everyone on the plane. It was a touching moment and made me believe that most people still respect and honor our soldiers. I was pleasantly surprised that all the passengers remained in their seats until this young man exited the airplane.

Jeanne
New Manchester, W. Va.

This past weekend my wife and I were dining at a very expensive restaurant for which we had received a gift certificate. Shortly after we were seated, a young Marine, his date, and five other couples were seated next to us. Having been a Marine twenty years ago, I could tell he had just gotten out of boot camp. I reminded my wife how I had been waiting for the day when I would see a new Marine in a restaurant. I wanted to pick up the tab, but my wife and I both knew we couldn't afford dinner for twelve in that place. Instead I spent our gift on appetizers for the table. My wife and I watched as these teenagers tried foods they never had before.

When the bill came, the waitress asked if it was okay to tell the young Marine who had sent the food. I said, "No. The food wasn't for him. It was for his friends—so they would know they were with some-one very special."

Lou
Catasauqua, Pa.

My husband and I head up a 4H club in Columbiana County, Ohio. We have twenty-one members ranging in age from nine to eighteen. Each year we do something to honor or support our troops. This past August, during our county fair, the Marines set up a display with a tank and some other equipment. The kids spend a lot of time at the fair because most of them have animals that they exhibit, so they had already checked out the Marines' display. We got together on the last day of the fair, bought milkshakes at the dairy bar, delivered them to the Marines, and offered our heartfelt thanks for what they do for all of us. The kids were awestruck talking to them and, of course, the Marines were as polite and humble as can be. A very uplifting experience for me!

In the past, as a club, we have also sent boxes of small gifts and letters to the vets in the hospital and snacks, supplies, and letters to Iraq through military connections.

There are a lot of little things you can do to show your appreciation to our troops.

Judy
Hanoverton, Ohio

Rose, I thought I would let you know about my daughter's Brownie troop. As you probably know, it's Girl Scout Cookie time. This Brownie troop sold approximately sixty boxes of cookies to send to our military serving overseas. Originally, the troop planned to use the Yellow Ribbon Girls to send the boxes; however, they were overloaded with cookies so they sent them through Trinity Episcopal Church. The girls who sold cookies for the military earned a service patch.

Elaine
Slippery Rock, Pa.

Two years ago I had the opportunity to travel through Shannon, Ireland, on my way to Europe (I stopped in Ireland to golf for a couple of days). While waiting for our plane, we made our way to the departure lounges and duty-free area of the airport.

Shannon has been a main stopping point for U.S. soldiers coming in and out of the Middle East. The area was full of hundreds of soldiers, half of whom were going home, half of whom were going to Iraq and Afghanistan.

The great thing is that they were all equally pumped up, whether coming or going. You couldn't tell the difference. Many were sitting at the bar drinking beer (at 9:30 a.m., by the way); others were floating around buying last-minute items. We spent a good hour and a half shaking hands, talking, and thanking them for their service—and we gave the bartender a few hundred dollars to help wet the soldiers' whistles.

We smiled for three days. What a credit to the United States these soldiers are.

Robert
Pittsburgh, Pa.

I live just down the road from the small town of McConnelsville on the Muskingum River, home of the Hawk Missile Site. I bought some gas in town yesterday. As I started pulling out of the station I noticed a soldier pumping gas. Immediately I backed up, parked, and went inside and asked if he was paying with cash or credit card. Fortunately, he was paying with cash. So I gave the attendant ten bucks to cover at least part of his gas (I didn't have much cash on me). I received a smile from the young man behind the counter that conveyed he understood exactly why I was supporting the soldier. From the look on his face, I suspect this happens frequently in this patriotic little town.

When I got home, I reported to my wife in the presence of my children what had transpired. I explained to my family that these fine men and women who serve in the military pay for our freedom. The least I could do was pay for this man's gas. Wow, did that feel good! Thanks for planting the seed. I can't wait to do it again.

Greg
Beverly, Ohio

I own a beer-distributor business in Clairton, Pennsylvania. If an Iraqi returnee is from anywhere in the Mon Valley, he has a case of beer waiting for him on me.

I do this for any serviceman that comes into my store who has returned from Iraq. I've given out about fifteen cases of beer in the last year.

Jack
Clairton, Pa.

Rose, I especially enjoy your radio show's segments about everyday citizens helping out the members of our military. Today I got a chance to do my part! I run the service department at a Chrysler-Dodge dealership in northern New York. Yesterday a 2005 Chrysler PT Cruiser was towed into our shop with some type of manual-transmission failure. Upon investigating the cause, we found that the clutch plate had broken. Unfortunately for the owner, a clutch is considered normal wear and not covered under any warranty—and to make matters worse, his warranty had expired anyway.

At this point we had not even met the owner because the vehicle was towed without him. My service advisor worked up a price for the customer and called him with a quote of $748 for replacement of the clutch. Today the owner showed up at the dealership dressed in his U.S. Navy uniform. He was a fairly young guy, about thirty-five years old. He explained that he was just transferred to the area from Virginia and that he wasn't due to be paid until sometime next week. He didn't cuss or swear about the price of the repair, but it was obvious to me that he was in serious doubt about coming up with the money at all. He gave approval for the repair and left the dealership before I got to speak with him again.

Seeing that young man in uniform struggling to determine how he was going to pay for this repair immediately sent my brain into overdrive to figure out a way we could help him. I don't have the authority to allow the dealership to eat the cost of repairs, so I called my Chrysler rep and explained that I had a low-mileage vehicle, out of warranty, with an unusual clutch failure. I said that the owner was a member of the Navy and I would like to help the guy if I could. My rep, Gary, didn't even hesitate in telling me: "Take care of the entire repair." Gary, like me, has the same appreciation for the members of the military; and although I placed the call, he authorized the Chrysler goodwill repair. I thanked him for feeling the same way that I did about the issue.

I then called the car's owner and explained that we had made arrangements for the vehicle to be repaired at no charge to him. The young man was speechless. He thanked me over and over again. I told him all I did was place the phone call and Chrysler did the rest.

Rose, I can't tell you how wonderful it is knowing that you've just helped one of our military out. It was difficult maintaining my emotional composure as I was telling him what we were doing and why. I thanked him for his service several times, and he was so appreciative of our gesture that I don't know if he realized how appreciative I was for his service to our country.

I feel good that I was able to help this guy out, even if it wasn't my money.

Dale
Corinth, N.Y.

Rose, after listening this morning to your program on my way to work, I enjoyed your sharing what others have done for our soldiers. You asked for more stories, so here is mine. I am the postmaster of Canton, Ohio—the Football Hall of Fame city. One day I went to my main-office lobby and observed a female customer with two small kids attempting to stuff a box full of items. I walked over to her to see if I could assist, only to discover that she was sending her husband, over in Iraq, a package of goodies. I helped with what I could and then walked to my clerk at the counter and gave him twenty dollars to cover her mailing expenses. It ended up just shy of that amount. I asked her to thank her husband for his sacrifice on behalf of all of us.

Bill
Canton, Ohio

I travel around the state frequently as part of my job as a Youth for Christ staff member. A few months ago at a Subway restaurant near Harrisburg, Pennsylvania, I had the opportunity to buy lunch for a soldier. She was just about to pay for her food when I offered to cover the check. She hesitated and looked at me rather awkwardly. I quickly realized that this might be an uncomfortable situation for her, since she was probably in her early twenties and a nice-looking young woman. I had to come up with a good follow-up to diffuse a potential problem. My solution was to mention my wife. I told her that I couldn't wait to get home and tell her that I bought lunch for a soldier. It was obvious that put her mind at ease and she allowed me to pick up the tab.

When I got home I did tell my wife about the incident. She asked if I would have bought the lunch if it had been a male soldier. The answer was yes.

Don
McMurray, Pa.

A couple of years ago, I was working in a local smoke shop. I was there with two of my regular customers when a couple walked in and said they wanted to buy some cigars to send to their son, a Marine in Iraq. They said they wanted something inexpensive because things were a little tight. I took them into the humidor, explaining that I would give them a discount for their son's service. I showed them several good selections, and on the way out I grabbed a handful of expensive cigars with the intent of giving them to the couple with a humidor bag in which they could ship them.

Interestingly, without a word between us, my two customers had had the same idea. Both had picked out ten very expensive cigars, paid for them, and told me to give them to the couple for their son. Both customers then left. When the couple brought out their purchases they were surprised to learn of the generosity of their fellow Americans. Both became teary, which also got me a little misty. The mother hugged me and thanked me up and down. I told her that her son was the one who deserved the thanks.

Tom
Pittsburgh, Pa.

I had my first opportunity to buy dinner for military members this evening. What an experience.

I was in Charleston, West Virginia, on business and went into a Texas Roadhouse restaurant on the way back to the hotel. When I sat down at a booth I noticed a table of five people—three men and two women; two of the men were wearing military camouflage. When my waitress came to my booth I asked her if she was waiting on the table with the military guys. She said she wasn't. So I requested that she have their waitress come see me.

A little later another waitress came up and I asked her if they were all together or if they had requested separate checks. She said that they requested separate checks. I told her that I wanted to cover the meals of the military guys. She said that they were all military. Without hesitating I said I wanted to cover all of them (trusting, of course, that my wife would understand because I had no idea how much it might be). The waitress got the most appreciative look on her face and said, "I was hoping someone would." She said that another gentleman had picked up their first round of drinks, and also that her fiancé was stationed at Fort Bragg and was going to be deployed to Iraq this summer.

She brought their check to me instead of delivering it to their table. A few minutes later all five of them came over to my booth and thanked me in the most sincere manner I have ever experienced. I told them all that I was the one who was thankful for their willingness to serve. Some had tears in their eyes, and I know I did. They went back to their table and finished their drinks while I was eating my dinner. When they got up to leave they came past my booth to thank me again. I tell you, I had trouble finishing my steak.

I consider myself a generous giver to charity, but nothing was as rewarding as the sincerity of those five soldiers in their thanks. God bless them.

Duane
Wooster, Ohio

I am a very proud American who works hard for everything I have. If I take a day off, it's Friday, but usually I work at least half that day and take a coworker or client to lunch and end early.

Last Friday I went to a local restaurant and noticed a young Marine and his lady having lunch. I finished about the time they got their food, so I approached our server and told her that I would like to pick up their check.

She looked at me like I was nuts! When I insisted, she told me that he was about to be deployed and she was a friend of his and of his girlfriend. I insisted on remaining anonymous and told her to thank him for his service. I can't remember the last time I felt better. I was on cloud nine the rest of the day. I did not go back to work.

Can't wait to do it again. God bless America and all the men and women who keep us free!

Don
Southwestern Pa.

I've been disappointed that I never seem to run into a member of the military while shopping or at a restaurant. So I came up with a different way to thank a service member.

I drive a lot in my work and sometimes see a house all decorated with flags and a sign reading something like "Welcome Home, Bill." I keep a fifty-dollar supermarket gift card in my car, and when I see one of these homes, I can put the card in an envelope addressed to "Bill" and thank him for his service. I just drop it off ... and boy, does it make me feel good.

I hope you can share this idea with your listeners to expand your thank-you efforts.

Diane
Pittsburgh, Pa.

I have a "soldier story" that has probably happened to others. My wife and I were at an area restaurant when I noticed a soldier sitting in the bar area; I asked the waitress if she would bring him a beer and charge it to my tab. She was a very young lady and looked at me rather quizzically but went about the task anyway. She came back a moment later and asked me which soldier I wanted to buy one for. From where we were sitting I did see that his whole team was back there! Well, I told her, buy them all one. It was a well-spent twenty-five dollars.

Alan
Steubenville, Ohio

I'm a pilot for a U.S. airline and I was recently passing through Detroit. We had an extra fifteen minutes or so to burn, so I stopped by the McDonald's in the terminal to grab a bite before my flight.

In line in front of me was a soldier in desert camo. I started chatting with him a bit—the usual small talk—and when it came to his turn, I moved up next to him and added my order to his, stating to him and the cashier that I had both covered.

He protested initially, saying, "You don't have to do that." I simply stated, "You're doing enough already." He thanked me, took his meal, and went to a table.

I sat down with the soldier and he had lots of airplane questions that I enjoyed answering for him (he wants to be a pilot), and then we went our separate ways.

After he left and as I was leaving, I noticed my receipt was a little low. I looked down the itemized list and saw that while everything was on there, they gave me a 50 percent discount (airport employees usually get 10 or 20 percent off, depending on the vendor).

I went back to the register and asked the cashier about the discount. I told him, "You gave me a 50 percent discount instead of the usual one." He replied, "Yeah, I know," adding, "Can't I play too?"

I laughed and thanked him for his generosity. Usually when you give, it comes back ... but not so quickly!

Here's another one for you.

About three or four times per year, I'll treat myself to a professional massage. Well, today was one of those days.

While waiting for my appointment, I heard one of the receptionists taking an appointment over the phone. After she hung up, she told the other receptionist that this was the third call she'd had recently from a soldier's wife who was making an appointment because her husband was coming home from Afghanistan or Iraq.

After my appointment, I stopped at the counter and told them that I couldn't help but overhear the conversation about the latest call from a soldier's wife. I asked if the woman was getting him a massage. She said it was for the wife—she wanted to have her hair and nails done for him right before he got home. As I was paying for my service, I told the receptionist to prepay that woman's service on my card as well.

Unfortunately, I'll never get to see who it was or her reaction (or her husband's), but the thought of her wanting to look her best for him when he returned home was touching.

The opportunities to thank these guys are out there if you're watching and listening for them.

Jeff
Medina, Ohio

Rose, listening to your stories of giving to soldiers during the Christmas season has inspired me more than I can say. My son is currently coming to the end of his third tour in Iraq, and since I keep track of his finances for him while he's away I certainly know how much (or should I say how little) money our men and women in uniform earn.

So, while listening to you tell stories of good deeds that people have done for the soldiers, I decided that I wanted to do something to show how much we appreciate our troops and to honor my son for everything he has given.

Before Christmas I picked up ten gift cards. My intent was to randomly give them to soldiers or Marines as I was doing my Christmas shopping. I didn't find a single one.

Then I decided to go to the airport, hoping to find soldiers—but everybody I saw was behind the security barrier and I could not get to them. By Christmas Day, I still had ten gift cards and hadn't found a single soldier or Marine. I was so disappointed. So I decided to keep them and during the year pass them out if I crossed paths with anyone in uniform.

This past Friday night my other kids and I took my husband to the Washington Capitals hockey game for his birthday. As we were walking through the arena before the game, I found four soldiers standing at a recruiting booth. And guess what? My gift cards were in the car down in the garage. Not to be deterred, I went back to the garage, got the cards, and went in search of soldiers. I found the four soldiers at the recruiting booth and approached them to thank them for their service.

After shaking hands with each of them and telling them about my son, I gave each of them a gift card. They were thrilled.

I can't begin to tell you how wonderful I felt— like Santa Claus in February. My kids thought I was so cool that they wanted in on the act. I gave them a couple of cards and during the break they found another soldier outside and gave him a gift card too.

Later, during the hockey game, they showed a soldier, who had been at Walter Reed, on the telescreen. He was sitting with his wife and two small sons in a luxury box. After he received a standing ovation from the crowd for almost a minute, I discovered that he was sitting just below us. I made my way to his suite and, to his embarrassment, gave both his sons gift cards to Best Buy. He was shocked and so thankful.

We do not hear much about the good our troops do these days, and they get so little in return for their protection of this country. I'm purchasing more gift cards and will keep on distributing them whenever I see a soldier or Marine throughout the year. Thank you so much for inspiring me.

Jeryl Ann
Berkeley Springs, W. Va.

Today I was in a Barnes & Noble store in Ashland, Ohio, standing in front of a woman who was in the Air Force. She was talking with my two-year-old daughter, Katharine, asking her name and being very friendly—she had the same name as my daughter. I don't have a lot of money but I had a gift card with a couple of dollars on it; I gave it to the cashier and told him to put it toward her bill. I was so embarrassed at the small amount that I scooted out of there as quickly as possible with my two-year-old. I just hope she did not think I was being cheap.

Dianna
Ashland, Ohio

I am a housewife who has a small part-time job at a little Italian grocery store in my community. I decorate cakes.

This summer I got an order for a big cake for

a local Marine who was coming home from Iraq. I decorated it with the Marine insignia and a map of the United States and a big "Welcome Home." Then I paid for it (because I'm part-time—I am not usually there when the cakes are picked up). I wrote a note to thank this young man for keeping us safe and express how very proud we are of him. I have no idea who this young man is and I have never met him, but I can tell you that it felt great letting him and his family know how much we appreciate his service.

I have never told anyone this, except my husband. Just wanted to share it with you.

Tina
Yatesboro, Pa.

I wanted to pass this along since it is a good example of the American Spirit!

I played hooky from work a little on Friday morning to take my wife out to breakfast. As we were finishing our meal, a couple of military gentlemen in fatigues sat at a table immediately behind us. This prompted some discussion between my wife and I about supporting our troops and how important this was. When our waitress came back with our check, I asked if I could also please have the check for the two brave Americans sitting at the next table as well. To my surprise, she told me that she could not do that, because someone else in the restaurant had already picked up their check. It warmed my heart!

Not wanting to leave things alone, my wife and I agreed that we would purchase a twenty-five-dollar gift card for the two men so that next time they stopped for breakfast it would be taken care of, just in case no other individuals were treating them to a meal.

Doug
Canal Fulton, Ohio

My wife and I had a layover in Atlanta on our way back to Williamsburg, Virginia. While eating lunch we met and had a great conversation with a young serviceman from Virginia who was soon to be heading back to Iraq. Our conversation with him caused me to realize how our media's coverage of the war makes it sound worse than it really is.

Prior to leaving the restaurant we paid for his meal and told him that we were proud of him and of all the others in uniform serving our country and fighting for our freedom.

I know this is a very small part of the big picture. But I felt really good inside after talking to this young man.

Craig
Williamsburg, Va.

I travel about once a month and many times have to fly. Recently, in the Atlanta airport while waiting for my plane, I noticed a young soldier in uniform walking up to a bank of pay phones. After trying to get all six of them to work, which he could not, the young soldier looked a little bewildered. So, I offered him my cell phone and told him to use it for whatever he needed.

A few years ago and before listening to your efforts to bring this to the listeners' attention, I might not have done a thing. But I felt both the obligation to help as well as the pride to be able to do something for these brave young men who do so much for us every day. His calls did not cost me anything as my cell plan has free long-distance calling, but the young man was very grateful and left the area with a large smile on his face.

Many thanks to you for keeping this in front of us.

Bruce
Allison Park, Pa.

We visited our son and his family in the Toledo, Ohio, area last weekend. As we left for home, we went to an ice cream shop called Maggie Moo's—our grand-daughter's name is Maggie, which was why we picked it. As we were enjoying our ice cream, we saw a soldier come in and get in line. My husband went to the lady taking the money and told her he wanted to pay for the soldier's food. She told him it wasn't necessary—that anything purchased by active military this month is "on the house." We thought it was great. I'd never heard of Maggie Moo's before, and don't know if they have other locations and if all their stores are doing that, but I wanted to recognize this one.

Anne
Navarre, Ohio

This comes from our son, who lives in Toledo. It warmed my heart, and I know it will yours as well. I told him I would send it on to you.

"I hope this note finds you well and in good spirits—if not, maybe it will help cheer you up. Our neighbor Chris is home on twelve-day leave from Iraq. Jim and Carol picked him up at the airport last night and took him out to eat at Loma Linda's. When they got there, the place was packed. The hostess asked them how many, and then, seeing Chris in his fatigues, asked if he was home from Iraq. Yes, he said. So she replied, 'You are not waiting.' Their

party of six got seated immediately in the packed
restaurant. After getting seated, the hostess announced over the P.A. system: 'Chris is a sergeant
home from Iraq. Why don't we all give him a round
of applause?' Instant standing ovation from everyone
in the place! Jim lost count of how many people
came up to shake Chris's hand and thank him. After
they finished their dinner and were getting ready to
leave, the hostess again, over the P.A., asked for one
more round of applause for Chris. Another standing
ovation. I wish I could have been there to see it—
must have been really something."

Anne

We had an opportunity last night to thank a soldier
and his family. We decided to use a gift card that had
been given to us for an Olive Garden restaurant in
Canton, Ohio. We arrived and were told the wait
would be an hour—not unusual there. As we began
our wait, we noticed a soldier with his wife and two
daughters also waiting. So we decided that we would
give our gift card to them through one of the servers
and instructed her to thank him for his service. She
did. Then a seat next to me in the waiting area became vacant, and one of the soldiers' daughters
asked if she could sit there. Of course I welcomed
her gladly.

Eventually the whole family was close to us, so we could tell him "Welcome home" and find out that he had arrived home *that day* from his second tour in Iraq. We sat and visited with this wonderful couple and their little girls (who were hanging all over their dad) for about a half hour. He'd been in Mosul for a year. He recently came very close to being killed. Some of the humvees are equipped with protection against the roadside bombs, but some are not. As they were traveling through a particular area, he was in the lead vehicle (with four of his men), which did not have that protection. His lieutenant and three others in another vehicle said that they would take the lead since they did have the protection. They did—but all four of those men died in an explosion; the protection didn't help. The wife of this soldier said that the four men in her husband's vehicle had fifteen children altogether. All of those children would have been fatherless had it not been for the action of that lieutenant. In the lieutenant's vehicle, only one was a father. Not to diminish the loss, of course; the soldier's wife has corresponded with the mother of that child to offer their deep gratitude.

We expressed to this couple how we wish the media would let us know about the heroes and all the wonderful work they are doing there. We mentioned your show and how you and others like you support our military. We noticed that during our meal, the Olive Garden staff sang a "celebrate" song to the family. And, as we were leaving, the waitress to whom we had given the gift card thanked us, in tears, for what we had done. We left wondering where the hatred is for our military that we are told exists.

So, thank you for encouraging all of us to do something to thank those who serve so bravely, sacrificing so much. I wish you could have seen this young man—so clean-cut and handsome. He's a "lifer," having already served fifteen years in the Army. I will have his face in my mind when I pray for our troops' safety at night.

Anne

I have a small thing to add to your list of things that are being done for our troops. My son goes to a public middle school and they had a soldier tree. The students who wished to participate brought home a stocking from the tree with directions to fill it with suggested items and return it to school. The stockings were then shipped to soldiers overseas. In addition, there is a spot on our son's Boy Scout order form so that you can have a gift delivered to military families. We gladly participated in both!

Amy
Washington, Pa.

We are all cigar smokers. When the Drew Estates Cigars rep showed up at Bloom Cigar Co. in Pittsburgh's South Side, they told him about our friend's son, who is in the service. The company sent the soldiers cigars, hats, shirts, and more as a thank-you from home.

Carol
Connellsville, Pa.

I wanted to relate what we did the other day when my husband and I were at a truck stop in Louisiana. We had to stop there to weigh our load before going on with it. Inside there is a restaurant. Waiting in line for a table were eight soldiers. Once we got our load weighed we went back into the restaurant and saw that they had ordered. We went to the waitress and said that we wanted to take care of their bill. Once that was done we went to their table and thanked them all for what they are doing for this country. Before we left we said, "Oh, by the way, lunch is on us." The look on their faces was of shock, then smiles. They yelled thanks as we left. It was a great day!

The next day we were finally able to go home and found a surprise waiting for us. You see, for the last few months we have been sending care packages to our neighbor, Helen, who is in Iraq. Waiting on our porch was a package for us—an American flag! She had had it flown over Iraq in our honor on Christmas Day. What a terrific surprise that was! We have great men and women over there.

Brenda
Saucier, Miss.

Good afternoon, Rose. I listen to your show as much as I can due to my work schedule. A few weeks ago I heard you talking about paying for our guys in the military—meals and gas, etc. I was at a gas station and talked to a military mom whose son had just come back from Iraq. Though he wasn't there I gave her money for gas and said to thank him for his service. Thanks for the idea!

Johnathan
New Tripoli, Pa.

I recently had the honor and pleasure to video-record the wedding of two Army veterans (from the Iraq war). As my gesture of appreciation for their service, I post-produced (edited) their entire wedding video at no charge to them.

Myles
Wexford, Pa.

My family and I were out for an easy bite to eat at a local pizza restaurant when a small group of Marines came in. Since you pay first there, we couldn't pick up the tab. Instead, we sent over our four-year-old son with some money and he handed it to the one man and said, "Thank you for your service." My husband promptly followed up, saying, "We couldn't buy the food so go have a few drinks on us."

The servicemen didn't seem to know what to do, other than say thanks and smile at the boy. We explained to my son as we were leaving that they were Marines like his grandfather and they were fighting to keep us safe.

We were thanking them, we told him, and he should always thank any servicemen and servicewomen he sees because they are volunteering to do something really important.

Emily
North Huntington, Pa.

Sometime Saturday, this past July, I was on my way
to work. I stopped at a gas station in Washington,
Pennsylvania. I had to prepay for gas before I could
pump it into my car. So I walked into the building and
over to the cold-drink area and got myself a cola.
When I got to the register, I saw a soldier in his twenties wearing his Army uniform. I saw he had a can of
Skoal and he was digging through his wallet for
money to pay. I reached past him to the clerk and
told the clerk his bill was on me.

The clerk stared at me with a puzzled look on
his face. So I said to the clerk, "I am paying for the
soldier's items as well as mine." The soldier said,
"No, I have it." I looked back at him and told him that
I was paying for his stuff to thank him for serving our
country. He seemed shocked and surprised, and he
thanked me.

Afterward, as he took his things and walked
away, the cashier smiled at me and said, "That was
nice; you're a good man." That meant a lot, and I
hope I am a good man. I, like my father and uncle,
served the country. My father was in the U.S. Marine
Corps. I was in the U.S. Army.

My father and I were at a WVU football game
last year. The announcer on the intercom system
asked all veterans to please rise. So my father and I
stood up. For me it was awesome, to stand there

with my dad, a man I looked up to as a kid, and being a veteran just like him. We were looking around at all the veterans standing in the stadium, and people were applauding them all. As we sat down, a man and his wife sitting next to us shook our hands and thanked us for our service.

I never thought a lot about serving when I did. It was my job and I wanted to do it well. That was the same for my father. The Toby Keith song that says, "I didn't do it for the money, I just did it anyway" is so true. After the man and his wife thanked us, I looked at my father and I said, "That always chokes me up when someone thanks me." My dad looked back at me and said that it was the same for him.

I have three kids of my own now—two daughters and a son. My wife and I are planning on having one more. I have felt torn because I feel obligated and I want to return to serving my country, but my age and the shape I'm in make me a little nervous.

My wife and mother have told me that I have served and that there are other people doing it now. I guess my patriotic side feels it's my duty to return. Although I love my current job and have taken my wife's advice, I still feel obligated. I love my country and I love my home state.

Paul
Southwestern Pa.

Here is a true story about one man's opportunity to
say thanks to America's finest. John loves this country and is in awe of our military. As the manager of
the service department for a small family-owned
business in Bridgeville, Pennsylvania, John was hiring a new mechanic. He sent out an e-mail sharing
news of a recent hire. Here is the story in John's own
words.

"I have some wonderful news. I have had the
honor and privilege of hiring a United States Army
veteran who was wounded by an RPG (grenade) in
active combat in Iraq. He served for ten years and
had one side of his face blown off. He is okay today
and the surgeons did an incredible job on him. He is
out of the Army now, fully recovered and doing very
well. He was a drill sergeant for a while and also
helps families of wounded veterans cope with their
loved ones who have been wounded. It has been one
of the greatest experiences of my career to be able
to meet this young man and offer him employment.
He has an aura about him that is incredible. He is always smiling and pleasant. God bless him and thank
God for sending him our way."

John is my husband and I can tell you that he
comes home from work every day beaming and full
of excitement over Michael, the Army veteran he
hired. John truly feels he is the lucky one in this
story. He cannot serve his beloved United States, but

he has been given an opportunity to say thank you
to someone who has.

Karen
Avella, Pa.

A few years ago, Amy (a colleague of mine in the history department of our local high school) informed
us that her husband, Brian (a Kentucky National
Guard member), would be coming home from his
second tour of duty in Iraq. She told me and another
colleague, Randy (with whom I also go to church),
that she wanted to do something special for Brian
for their anniversary, which would be shortly after
he returned home. So, Randy and I said we would
mention this as a service project to our Bible study
group.

Our study group was thrilled to jump at the opportunity. So, after finding out that Brian had always
wanted a flagpole in his front yard, Amy ordered the
flagpole and requisite American flag. All twelve members of our study group (with help from Lesley, another member of the history department, and her
husband) planted flowers and shrubs, and remulched
their flowerbeds. We also dug the hole for the flagpole,
poured the concrete, ran the line for a light to shine
on the flag, and hoisted the flagpole and flag.

We were all exhausted—but it was well worth our efforts when Brian came home. He was very excited and emotional when he saw the new addition to their yard. Brian thanked all who helped on the project for their time and generosity, and for looking after his family while he was in Iraq. I told him that that doing this for him and his family was our way of thanking them for their sacrifices.

Ryan
Hartford, Ky.

Rose, I would like to thank you for the inspiration to thank our soldiers. My daughters and I had an opportunity one day to do just that. We drove into a local restaurant drive-thru to place an order. When I pulled up to the window to get our food I noticed what appeared to be a solider behind us in line. I explained to the lady at the window that I wanted to pay for my order and that of the person behind me. She looked at me strangely and asked why would I want to do that. I explained that I wanted to "Thank a Soldier." The lady was stunned at first and then told me that it was a very kind gesture. My daughters, ages six and nine, wondered why I would pay for someone else's stuff. I explained to them that the soldiers give up everything, including their lives, for

our freedom and it is the least we can do to pay for
their order. Since that day my daughters are always
on the lookout for military personnel. I think it is a
great lesson to teach the younger generations of this
country to appreciate those who sacrifice everything so that they can have decent lives. Hopefully
this lesson will stay with my daughters as they
grow up.

Samantha
East McKeesport, Pa.

At the beginning of the summer, I noticed that a
home at a local four-way stop was sporting a new
sign. The sign was a welcome home to a soldier who
was apparently returning from his tour in Iraq. Upon
seeing the sign I decided to take the opportunity to
thank this individual. I made a small detour and
stopped at a chain store, where I picked up a card
with an image of the globe on the front and a simple
"Thank You" on the inside. I wrote in the card:

"I know you don't know me, and we probably
will never meet face to face. I just want you to know
that my family and I thank you. I thank you not only
for your service, but for what it means—the differ-
ences you have made here and the freedoms that
you, and those who serve, allow us to have. Thank

you for the improvements you make possible all
around the world, and the actions that you may
never be thanked for but for which we all know you
should be thanked. So, for all those who couldn't, or
were too shy to, express their gratitude, and for all
those you've helped and who don't even know it—
Thank you and God bless you."

David
Masontown, Pa.

My name is Dan and I'm an instructor at a technical
school. A good friend of my daughter (we'll call her
Mickie) touched our family in a very unique way. Her
father is active military and was being deployed to
Iraq. A few days before he was to leave, they were
going to celebrate Mick's birthday. She was so excited, since she was going to get her iPod. Well, the
day before, their water heater broke and the birthday money went to fix the heater—no iPod.

A couple of days after Mike deployed, a supermarket gift card showed up in their mailbox for the
same amount as an iPod. I wanted to just give her
the device, but that particular gift was probably special to the parents as their gift to the girl.

I believe everything happens for a reason and
the Big Guy has a plan for all of us—so I just waited

for the correct time to thank this family for the sacrifices they are making for us. Then it happened. Mike (Mickie's dad) had come home. And all was good.

Mike called me and explained that his car had stopped running (it needed an engine). Well, without hesitation I agreed to have my students install an engine in his car. He was told by a GM dealer that repairs would be around four thousand dollars. Well, the whole job was done for just about seven hundred dollars. I was so excited when the job was finished that I couldn't wait to call Mike and let him know he could pick up the car.

I wanted to do this for them as a thank you for what they have done for us, and I was amazed when he said that he was the one who was thankful, thankful that we were willing to help when we were asked to. And that is the greatest reward I have ever received. If I ever have the opportunity to offer help like this again, I will not hesitate to step up to the plate.

Dan
North Huntington, Pa.

Rose, you will remember the story of a car engine that my students and I installed a while ago for a member of our military. It was my son's graduation party yesterday, and through all of the chaos associated with the preparations, I was taken somewhat by surprise when I noticed Michael (a military member) standing behind me. I was completely overwhelmed when he presented me with an American flag, folded neatly in the traditional triangle, encased in a beautiful display case.

Accompanying the flag were two certificates documenting that the flag was flown in combat over Afghanistan on board a B-1B bomber in support of Operation Enduring Freedom on May 19, 2010. This flag was also flown by the 171st Air Refueling Wing, which was redeploying troops from Al Udeid Air Base in Qatar to Pittsburgh. Not only was this flag flown in combat and presented to me, it was flown in honor of my family for helping him out some time ago.

With tears in my eyes, I must tell you that I have always treasured being an American, and have always been aware of the sacrifices our military makes every minute of every day to maintain our freedom. I asked Michael why he did this. His reply was very direct and caused an instant welling up of emotion in me. He said, "Because you support us." To be thought of in this fashion is incredible, and to see this flag on my mantle every day will be a reminder of just how blessed we are.

Dan

With all of the negative publicity that our Armed Forces members receive in the press, I'd like to share a positive story with you.

Last Thursday, December 13, I was on a flight to Pittsburgh from Dallas, Texas. One of the passengers was a young soldier dressed in her fatigues. As we began our descent into Pittsburgh, the flight attendant announced that we had a special passenger aboard who was returning to Pittsburgh after serving ten months in Iraq. The entire plane burst into applause and cheers for her. The flight attendant suggested that we honor the young soldier's service by letting her be the first to deplane.

As we rolled down the runway and pulled into the gate, all the passengers remained seated. The flight attendant smiled and motioned for the private to come forward to deplane. All the passengers looked to the rear of the plane and watched as the soldier made her way down the aisle. Everyone clapped, shouted "Thank you for your service," and cheered her out of the plane. That's how Americans really feel!

Pat
Gibsonia, Pa.

I just returned from a family vacation in Myrtle Beach. It was a bittersweet vacation since we were returning my oldest son to South Carolina as he starts back to school. While on the coast, we enjoyed some of the best Calabash seafood the area had to offer. My children got our money's worth at the all-you-can-eat crab-leg buffets, and they probably lost a couple of bucks on my meal as well. Every day it seemed like our biggest decisions were what and where to eat breakfast, lunch, and dinner. We enjoyed plenty of beach activities and attractions, but the highlight of the trip seemed to be the food.

While we were driving back to Ohio, we recapped all of the meals we enjoyed, and my younger (ten-year-old) son asked everyone what their favorite meal of the trip was. We relived the lobster at one place, or the bruschetta at another. When it came back to him, I asked him what his favorite was. His reply was that the best dinner was the one he didn't eat. Confused, I asked him what he was talking about. Apparently somewhere in West Virginia, my wife went up to the counter at a restaurant on our way home and picked up the tab for a soldier who was dining alone in the booth behind me. My son witnessed this and asked her about it. She explained to him why she was honored to treat the soldier to dinner. My son listens to the War Room with us on occasion and recognized this as Rose's "thing from the show." My wife set a great example for him—and hopefully for anyone else within earshot. And you guys set a wonderful example for listeners across the country every day.

John
Akron, Ohio

A few months ago my wife and I were having lunch at a local Red Lobster restaurant. A young soldier and his family (his wife and two children) were sitting next to us. I asked the waitress to put this family's meal on my bill. The soldier left before the bill arrived, but his wife and kids remained to settle the check. The waitress informed her that the bill had been paid. She teared up and thanked us, and then her children came over to give us hugs. We talked and I found out that her husband had just finished his second tour in Iraq and was going back in six months. I also discovered that the soldier's wife was expecting their third child, who would probably be born while her husband was overseas.

After the family left, the waitress came over and told us that she was so impressed by what we did that she was giving my wife and me free dessert!

Dan
Butler, Pa.

I was in Seven Springs, Pennsylvania, Saturday afternoon having lunch. Also dining was a family of three girls and a young man, with their great-grandmother. We were all listening to the DJ and dancing. The young man was quite a dancer. His sister informed the DJ that he was just back from Iraq. The DJ announced this and the crowd burst into rapturous cheering. The DJ asked the girls to line up and give him a hug or kiss. He was very humble and struggled to hold back tears. I bought him a beverage and gave him a man's hug as only men can hug each other. The look of awe in his eyes seemed to say, "How am I worthy of all this?" He had people coming up to him the rest of the afternoon and thanking him. Oh—and the line of girls giving him hugs and kisses ... wow!

Bob
Pittsburgh, Pa.

I have picked up the tab for several of our military. Each time it is gratifying, but one experience stands out.

I was at lunch during a recent business trip to Reading, Pennsylvania, with two business associates. We walked into a restaurant and I noticed two

Navy recruiters having lunch. As we sat down, I immediately told our server that I wanted the recruiters' bill along with ours. The two recruiters finished and then came over and said thank you.

After they left, both of the gentlemen with me—one of them a former soldier—commented that they thought buying the recruiters' lunches was a cool thing to do. One of my friends said, "I have heard about people doing this but I have never done it. You have inspired me to do it for another soldier." I said I thought it was the least we could do after all they have done for their fellow citizens. I hope he does follow through.

Chris
Toronto, Ohio

My first opportunity to help our brave men in uniform presented itself a little over a year ago. I was at a restaurant in the Portland, Oregon, area. Six soldiers came in and were seated at the table next to mine. One of my friends went over to address them, and when she came back she said, "I guess that was a mistake." When we questioned her, she said she thanked them for helping to defend our freedom and keep us safe. She said that several of them started crying. Needless to say, I didn't bother going over. I watched for their waitress and caught her out of their sight and gave her my credit card. When my friend found out what I did, she asked to split the bill with me, which I thought was terrific. They never knew who took care of their bill.

I have been blessed to have more opportunities to thank a soldier. Last September, I was in a Red Robin restaurant in the Seattle area at a business lunch. I spotted a couple of soldiers walk in but couldn't see where they were sitting. I walked around until I found them. They were at a table with two civilians. I hailed their waitress and gave her my credit card. She was a young girl and couldn't believe what I was doing. She was so excited. She said she couldn't wait to tell her dad what I did—she said her dad would probably want my autograph! I just chuckled, signed the receipt, and quietly left the restaurant.

I have friends who work at the Air National Guard base in Portland, and they told me about our F-15s being grounded this past December. As a result, pilots from other bases in California were sent to Portland to guard our base. They were stuck here over Christmas. I rolled up my sleeves and got busy in the kitchen. I made them cookies, four rum cakes, miniature cream puffs, and a couple of pumpkin rolls.

Since then, I've adopted a soldier through one of the many websites that match up sponsors with soldiers. I've sent him a goodie package and a few cards to date.

My niece has been in Iraq since February. I've now sent her two care packages and a few cards. I know she's having a difficult time being over there and is literally counting down the days until she can come home.

One other incident stands out. I was waiting in the Ontario, California, airport on Friday morning with coworkers. I walked away from them long enough to go over to a soldier and shake his hand and thank him for his service. He immediately expressed his gratitude for my support. Talk about an uplifting feeling!

I hope I will have many more opportunities to bless our heroes in the very near future.

Judy
Gresham, Ore.

My son, Joey, and I were traveling back recently from a karate tournament in Charleston, West Virginia, and he wanted to go to McDonald's for breakfast. Well, there were a number of Army convoys parked at the McDonald's. As we pulled into the parking space several of the military personnel were heading to their trucks with their bags of food. I quickly got out of the car, hoping to catch some inside.

Joey wasn't getting it—why I was in such a rush. I quickly explained that we had to try to thank them. He had this skeptical look on his face. At any rate, we went in and there were four military members at a booth and I approached them to thank them for their service. Joey watched. Then to another table, again thanking them while Joey watched. He excused himself to go into the restroom. While Joey was in the bathroom, I finally found a lone Army guy waiting to place his order. I eased on behind him, and after he placed multiple orders for his guys I waved the signal to the clerk and she smiled. He handed her his credit card and she handed it back. He initially declined to take my money but then graciously accepted. We engaged in small talk, and soon Joey approached us. Joey shook the soldier's hand and thanked him for his service. I thought my heart would burst—for the military, for my son (who had just become a man), and for our country, which is so blessed to have them.

Stacy
Bethel Park, Pa.

I am a middle-school language-arts teacher. Each class in our school will be completing an assignment that ties into the Presidential election. I have selected an assignment for my classes in which the students will be speaking in a narrative from a solder's point of view regarding this election. The students will research each candidate's positions on Iraq, military support, and other relevant issues.

As a service project to correspond with the narratives, my students have donated many items for a care package for our troops overseas. They were very excited and positive about the entire assignment. As a result, we have food and toiletries to send. The students did a great job and were extremely generous—some used their own money to purchase the items.

Tiffany
West Mifflin, Pa.

It was about five years ago, and my kids and I were in Mansfield eating at a restaurant. Three booths down, there were two National Guard soldiers and one active-duty soldier (he had a 101st Division patch on and desert cammies) eating lunch. I told the waitress that I would cover their bill and not to tell them who paid for it. Well, they finished eating and went to pay for the meal. You could tell they were surprised by the expressions on their faces (they were looking all around). My kids asked me why I did that. I told them that they have already paid for my freedom—I might as well pay for their lunch.

There are several reasons I didn't want them knowing it was me: I like to give quietly; I don't like praise; I do it because God wants me to; it makes me feel good; and I get very emotional when it comes to people who have served this country—I did not want to tear up in front of brave men when they thank me.

Tom
Holmesville, Ohio

I was at the NASCAR race in Dover, Delaware, recently. The soldiers were involved in the prerace festivities, as they always are at NASCAR races. The soldiers were outside the track, lined up and awaiting their cue to enter. As the cue was given and they began their march inside, hundreds of fans cleared a path for them, clapping and cheering as they made their way inside the track. Needless to say, it was a moving experience. Just another way we can thank our soldiers for all they do.

Gary
Level Green, Pa.

Last Saturday when I was finished grocery shopping at a local supermarket there was an Air Force reservist (in his fatigues) with his wife and two daughters going into the store as I put my cart in the cart rack. I got into my car and remembered I had gift cards up on my visor. I reparked my car and went back in and tracked the family down and gave the serviceman a hundred-dollar gift card; I said, "Thank you for your service to the country."

I felt pretty good until I remembered I had used one of the cards for gas the other day! I had to apologetically take it back; then I went to the Customer Service department and had the value checked. Fortunately, it was good for the hundred, so I tracked him down again and gave him back the card, with repeated thanks.

Greg
Warren, Ohio

My family and I were returning from vacation and we decided to stop at a restaurant in Robinson, Pennsylvania. Two tables away there was a group of six men dressed in desert fatigues, and I proceeded to tell my daughters that they are the reason that America is as great as she is.

After our waiter took our order I told him that my family was going to pay for the soldiers' lunches. We requested that the waiter only tell them it was from a family who really respects what they do for our country, and this was the least that we could do.

When the bill came I put my credit card into the holder to pay the waiter, and without a word my older daughter, Jessy, took twenty dollars out of her pocket (that is her money, as she has a car-cleaning business) and said she would like to pay for part of the bill. I had tears in my eyes because my girls get it and they are nine and fifteen.

Bill
Peters Township, Pa.

A few summers ago I was driving my daughter and her six children—my wonderful grandchildren—up to Lake Erie for a few days. We pulled off Interstate 79 to have breakfast at a restaurant. The eight of us were seated not far away from a soldier who was eating breakfast with his wife and two young children (I think they were around seven and nine).

I quietly told the waitress to give us their check and to thank the soldier for what he had done for us.

I had no idea how much it would mean to all of the children who had witnessed this. They were so proud of him. My grandchildren personally thanked him for his service. Tears filled his wife's eyes. I thanked her for supporting her husband and for both of their sacrifices. Tears welled up in the soldier's eyes now. My little grandson saluted him.

It was a wonderful learning experience for all of us, especially for our young impressionable ones.

Deborah
Southpointe, Pa.

While visiting a nationally known seafood restaurant in Pennsylvania's Washington County, my wife and I came across a family taking care of a young child whose mother was deployed to Iraq.

When we walked into the restaurant, we noticed a lady and a child sitting near the lobster tank. The young child was climbing all over the tank and was ... well, being a child. My wife sat down next to the woman and began to talk to both. My wife has a unique ability to engage any child in a comforting and calming discussion.

The child sat quietly and talked to my wife for twenty minutes. My wife learned the little boy was the son of the lady's best friend and his mother was deployed to Iraq. The young boy would not see his mother for three to four years. The boy told my wife he watches the news every night to see if his mother is all right.

Listening to this conversation simply broke me up. I noticed the rest of the woman's family was waiting outside. Periodically the young daughter and son would come in and whisper something to their mother. The family appeared to be celebrating a birthday, and this night out was something extraordinary. Finally their buzzer went off and they were seated.

We were seated ten minutes later and near their table. I asked their waitress to provide me with their check. The manager came over and quietly asked if he could split their check with me. I quickly said no, but told him he could pay for the next soldier or soldier's family that comes through the door. He agreed. My wife and I ate quickly, quietly paid their check, and left before they knew anything about it.

Boy, did we feel good during our fifteen-minute drive home. As a bonus, during the next few visits to that same seafood restaurant with the lobster tank in the lobby, the manager and a few waitresses came by our table to thank us for what we had done.

Brad
Eighty Four, Pa.

Rose, I did it! Several of my coworkers and I usually go out for lunch together on Mondays, and today we picked our local Pizza Hut. I happened to notice that two young Army guys were sitting a couple of tables away from us, so I quietly went up to the counter and asked the hostess for their bill; I also asked her not to tell them who paid it. When the servicemen were leaving, they came over to me and shook my hand, said thank you, and also gave all of us sitting there a bag of Army lanyards. I smiled and told them, "Thank you for your service." I guess the hostess couldn't keep my secret, but that's okay—it still made all of us feel pretty good.

One of the guys from my office said that this was the first time he'd ever seen someone else do that. He himself picks up the tab for service members quite often. I just told my coworkers what we always hear on your show: "They pick up the tab for us every day."

Karen
Duncansville, Pa.

There is a diner in my town where I eat lunch frequently. Often I would see this same elderly couple eating their meal. The man always wore a Screaming

Eagles (101st Airborne) hat and tee shirt. Judging by his age, I assumed he was a World War II vet. I always thought I'd like to ask him about his days in the 101st, but based on the look in his eyes and the way he was handled, I surmised he might have had Alzheimer's. Last Veteran's Day I stopped by the diner and gave the waitress enough money to cover their meal and tip; I asked her to tell them that their lunch was paid for by someone who appreciates the man's service to his country.

A few days later, I was eating at the diner and the couple walked in. I guess the waitress must have pointed me out to them, because the woman came to my table and thanked me. I wanted to let her know that even if her husband could no longer remember what he did for his country, others of us do.

When I was at the diner a few days ago, the waitress told me that the man had passed away. I didn't even know his name, but I'm sure he was one of this country's many unsung heroes. Thank God for them all!

Jay
East Liverpool, Ohio

I am currently staying near the Pittsburgh airport and got my hair cut tonight at Great Clips. The lady who cut my hair told me that her son has been in Afghanistan and yesterday two of his sergeants were killed by a suicide bomber. She then said her son was coming home tomorrow for two weeks for his brother's graduation party. She really worries about him being killed.

I usually tip fairly well, but I only put a $2 tip on my card for the $12 haircut because I knew what I was going to do. After I left I got $10 out of my car and went back in. I told her to use the money for dinner or something else with her son while he is home. She got all choked up. I left and then got teary eyed in the car. It really did make me feel good. I wish I had been able to give her more.

Joe
Indiana, Pa.

About one month ago, my family and I were eating lunch at a local fast-food chain restaurant. While we were eating, a young Army soldier walked in and placed his order. I immediately got up, stepped in front of him, and handed my bank card to the cashier: I asked her to place his order on my card. While she was processing his order, I thanked him and returned to my seat.

I could only muster a "thank you," as my

respect for these heroes runs so deep I was afraid I would break down in tears in front of everyone. The selflessness these brave men and women show for all of us—even those who openly rail against them—is one of the reasons that this country is the greatest one ever to be established on the planet.

For our soldiers to be fighting in Iraq and Afghanistan, to be away from their families, and to be willing to make the ultimate sacrifice for me and my children—all these things make them truly special people in my eyes.

Each of us owes these men and women much more than lunch. We owe them our thanks and unconditional support.

Keith
Zelienople, Pa.

I run a food-court operation at a local college. Every Veterans Day I try to buy a meal for a veteran. Considering where I work, it is extremely hard to find a vet, but I can often locate one among the local construction workers.

This Veterans Day a student walked up to my operation dressed in Army fatigues. As he came to the checkout I stared at him with an embarrassing look on my face and said, "Are you in the Army?" He said yes. I then asked, "Are you a for-real soldier?" He said, "Yes, I am." I told him that he didn't pay here. With a puzzled look he asked why. I said, "You are serving our country and I appreciate your service. Thank you." He still had a puzzled look on his face and thanked me and walked to a nearby table. As he stood at the table he was shaking his head, saying, "Holy cow, wow, geez," as if he never expected it. It made me feel like a million dollars—I was all choked up as I was talking to him.

Nick
Pittsburgh, Pa.

About two years ago I stopped to get my usual cup of coffee at a local convenience store when I noticed a young man in army fatigues in line in front of me. The first thing I did was thank the young man for serving for me and my county. Then I asked him if that bottle of water was all he was having for breakfast. He stated, "Yes, Ma'am." I stepped in front of him and told the cashier to ring it up with mine, and then turned and told the fellow that next time he should eat a better breakfast. Although he was a little embarrassed, the young man thanked me and held the door open for me, and we parted.

My story doesn't end there. Two weeks later, at

the day-care center where I was providing therapy for a client, the same young man, a single dad, came in to drop off his three-year-old daughter. I recognized him immediately and asked him if someone had bought him a bottle of water lately. He suddenly smiled with recognition and proceeded to tell me what happened after I had bought that bottle of water. His outfit was having a monthly staff meeting that day and he couldn't wait to share with the guys what had happened to him that morning. The guys were feeling less than appreciated thanks to the papers and news, and this soldier used this experience to improve the outfit's morale—all for the cost of a bottle of water. I paid it forward and so did he. That's what it is all about!

I have bought military guys lunch before, but this is the first time I ever got to hear how they had used the experience to boost the morale of others.

Juanita
Greensburg, Pa.

On a recent Saturday while my wife was working, I took my two young daughters to a Bob Evans restaurant for lunch.

As we were finishing our meal, a young man in a sailor uniform and a pretty girl were seated at a table right behind us. These young people had obviously not seen each other in a while—I think she had just picked him up from the airport—and it was clear they were very much in love.

When we went up front to pay for our meal, I told the cashier that I wanted to pick up their check, too. Well, she didn't know how to do that, so she had to get the manager. When the manager arrived, I told her what I wanted to do, and she was very helpful. She didn't say much, but she smiled and gave me a look of respect. The waitresses standing close by seemed a bit taken aback by the whole thing. I asked them to just tell the young man, "Thanks for your service."

We left anonymously, which was just fine with me. I figured it would be a nice surprise for this young couple. As we got into the car, my seven-year-old daughter asked me why I had done what I did. I explained to her that soldiers keep us safe and free, and that we should do nice things for them whenever we can.

I was thrilled to get my chance to do something—however small—for one of our Armed Forces members, and I know that the restaurant manager, a couple of waitresses, and my children all learned something that day!

Jerry
Winesburg, Ohio

I was in a convenience store and two Army Infantry soldiers walked in just behind me. I was there for a quick snack, and seeing them inspired me to step in front of them and tell the clerk that I would pay for whatever they wanted. Neither soldier was buying anything expensive—I think it was a refill from the soda fountain and a bottle of water—but it was terrific being able to shake their hands and thank them in whatever way possible. They both expressed their gratitude to me many times, but they are the ones who deserve the thanks. It was the least I could do.

Eric
Butler, Pa.

I was visiting my daughter in Chicago after she had surgery. I was having lunch downtown when four young sailors were seated at a nearby table. I paid attention to their order—colas and sandwiches. I can do this, I thought. I went up to the waitress and said, "Don't tell them, but I would like to pay for the sailors' meals." She went to her boss and then gave me their check.

I got out the door, but the boss evidently told them, because one of the young men came running out to thank us and offered to buy us a cab ride. He was such a baby-faced kid. I just thanked him for what he was doing and he went back into the restaurant.

What a pleasure it was to do have done something like this!

Ross
Gibsonia, Pa.

Two years ago, on a return trip from a hiking expedition, I came across an Army convoy returning from maneuvers. It was a hot day, over 90 degrees, and they were stuck in Army transport vehicles. I managed to get to the lead truck; yelling across, I found out how many were in the unit. I sped ahead to a local mini-mart and bought four cases of ice-cold pop and handed them to the guy in the lead truck. They all were so grateful to get something cold to drink. To add to this, when the mini-mart manager found out what I was going to do with the pop, he sold it to me at cost.

Mike
Pittsburgh, Pa.

Every time we visit a restaurant and my wife, Vicki, sees soldiers dining, she always buys their dinner. No big fuss: She quietly asks the server for their check, pays the tab, and then stops by and personally thanks the soldiers for their service.

At times I think she is going to send me to the poor house doing this. Whenever we enter a restaurant, I have to spy into the window to see how many soldiers are in there and then check my wallet to see if I have enough cash before we can enter!

Rick
Ravenna, Ohio

I won two hundred dollars in prepaid phone cards in a local game. Not knowing what to with them, I asked my wife. She said that we really don't need them. Then she said, "Let's give the phone cards to the troops in Iraq. I'm sure they could be helpful." We didn't know how to go about that, so she went to the local National Guard unit to ask. She was advised that several area troops were going over to Iraq later in the week and the prepaid cards would be given to them.

She was asked for her name so she could get

recognition for her deed. She said that wasn't necessary and then left.

When she came home, she talked about the warm, fuzzy feeling she had! I'm proud of our troops—and my wife.

Mike
Butler, Pa.

This is my first year running a small retail tax-prep shop in Niles, just north of Youngstown, Ohio. It seems our local Navy Reserve unit is on leave this week, and I had a few military members come in to have their taxes prepared. I'm sure you know where this is going—but they assuredly did not. I smiled to myself and proceeded as usual, telling them I would give them their tax-refund estimates and price quotes as soon as we went through our preliminary questionnaire and data entry. I figured out their taxes and had them sign their forms. I was well compensated for my work by the elation I saw in their eyes when I told them they wouldn't be paying for tax preparation services this year.

Even though we didn't meet our year's quota, I just felt it was my civic duty to help these soldiers in any way possible. While I couldn't pay them in cash, I was able to bless them with my services.

Rose, your show has done an outstanding job of inspiring our neighborhood patriots to pitch in a bit for our service members and our country. It is reminiscent of the old Victory Gardens, which were planted in the 1940s and allowed the U.S. government to buy large amounts of food for the war effort without the fear of starving our people at home. Every little bit of assistance we give the troops is a blessing upon them and our country as a whole.

Michael
Niles, Ohio

I was visiting my brother this summer in Denver and we were talking about the war. He is a businessman who flies several times a week. He told me this story.

Once he was sitting at the airport waiting for his flight, which was completely full, when he noticed a bunch of soldiers waiting for the same flight. He could tell they had just gotten back from Iraq. He went up to the group and asked them who was the most deserving of a first-class ticket. The group got real quiet and all pointed to one soldier. So my brother took that soldier up to the ticket counter and traded his own first-class ticket for the soldier's coach seat.

As the soldier sat in first class, my brother sat in coach with the other soldiers. He said that it was the best flight he ever took, because he got to hear stories about Iraq. He also asked one soldier why they had chosen that particular serviceman for first class. He said that he has a baby girl back home, and he has never seen her. My brother said they were the best group of guys he has ever met—and the first flight since 9/11 on which he has felt completely safe.

Patricia
Pittsburgh, Pa.

I was in Atlanta at Hartsfield-Jackson airport, waiting for a connecting flight. I saw a gentleman in his Army camo also waiting for his flight, so I offered to buy him breakfast. He graciously accepted. I told him he could have anything he wanted. He settled for a breakfast at one of the fast-food restaurants. After he ordered, and while we were waiting for his food to be prepared, he excitedly said that he had not had "good food" like this in months. He had been in Iraq for ten months, and was on his way home for a few weeks. I thanked him for his service, and went to my gate to wait for my flight. It was touching to see how excited he was to eat what was essentially greasy fast food that we Americans take for granted every day.

Zach
Cuyahoga Falls, Ohio

We were in the airport in Honolulu, Hawaii, waiting for our flight home when I overheard some men talking, only to realize that they were in the Marine Corps. So, I naturally interrupted and started talking with them about nothing other than the Pittsburgh Steelers! I found out that one Marine was from western Pennsylvania. As we talked, I also discovered that he had never been to a Steelers game. Being a fanatical fan, I could not let this young Marine serve our country, including going to Iraq, while never having gone to a Steelers game at Heinz Field.

Our family has been blessed and we have four club-level season tickets. So, I invited him and a guest to a game on behalf of our family, in thanks for his service to our country. This all took place in July, shortly after the Steelers had released the schedule, which I happened to have with me. I gave him the choice of any game, and he picked a Monday night game against the Ravens. We exchanged phone numbers, our flight was announced, and we left.

Several weeks later, I called the young Marine and reconfirmed his attendance. We talked one more time and then it was game day. He and his wife stayed at a hotel in Pittsburgh and we linked up with them there and passed off the tickets, along with some other Steelers goodies I had collected. Come game time, it was truly a great feeling for us to see the joy and excitement on the young Marine's face. Needless to say, the game was awesome and so was the time we were able to spend with one of America's true heroes!

Susan
Evans City, Pa.

Rose, I am a professional trucker who listens to your show on XM whenever I can. I don't know if anyone has told you what OOIDA (Owner-Operator Independent Drivers Association) is doing for our troops. In December they held a "telethon" for new and renewal memberships. From each new or renewed membership, $2.50 was put toward purchasing care packages for our troops in Iraq and Afghanistan. The association also matched the $2.50 for a total of $5 for each membership being donated. The goal was to raise $5,000 for the care packages. As a result of the memberships and straight cash donations by drivers, they raised over $40,000! The care packages will be sent out in February.

Scott
Jamestown, N.Y.

I was at the Pittsburgh airport approaching the long line at the security checkpoint. I saw a family saying goodbye to their son, who was in his military attire. They parted and he went to stand at the end of a very long line. I thought that he should not have to wait in line; so being a frequent flyer, I went over and told him to come with me. We walked through the first-class line (no waiting). I rode with him to the terminal and learned that he was getting ready to go to the Middle East. I wished him good luck and we went down our separate concourses.

About two days later, back at the office another associate of mine was recounting a story about a soldier who boarded his plane. My associate was in first class and the soldier was in coach. My associate walked back to the soldier and insisted he take his first-class seat. The other passengers cheered as the two switched seats. As we continued to share details of time and flights, we realized that it was the same solider I had escorted through the line. I guess we were meant to assist this young man as he departed to serve his country. It was a very small price to pay.

I also make it a practice to pick up the meals of soldiers I see in restaurants. I quietly ask the waitress to bring me the bill, and to not tell them who did it. I receive more blessings from this silent act of appreciation then you can imagine. God bless our soldiers.

Tom
Washington, Pa.

I didn't exactly thank a soldier, but I think I came close.

Tonight my wife and I went to our local Olive Garden restaurant for dinner. When our server came to the table, I noticed that she had a Blue Star pin on, as well as a yellow ribbon. When she left the table, I remarked to my wife that her brother must be serving in the military. I told her about the pin and explained that since she seemed kind of young and I didn't notice a wedding band, it must be for her brother.

As the meal progressed, I asked our server where her brother was. She gave me a puzzled look and asked me what I was talking about. I told her that I had noticed her pin and hadn't seen a ring. She showed me her wedding ring (apparently my sugar was low and my mind was only on pasta) and told us that her husband was in Anbar, and that he'd be home in seven weeks for two weeks, and then home for good in June.

When the check came, my wife told me to leave

her a good tip, because the guys in the military don't get paid enough. I did, about three times the bill. When she came back, I just handed her the receipt.

We put our coats on and headed for the door. Our server came up to us before we could get out of the dining room, and with tears in her eyes said, "You didn't have to do that." I told her that what her husband is doing for us is worth much more than that.

She asked if she could give me a hug, and then hugged us both. I headed for the door because I must have gotten something in my eyes, since they were starting to get rather damp. Man, what a feeling!

Wes
Cincinnati, Ohio

My company asked me to attend a meeting yesterday in Kingwood, West Virginia. After the meeting, three employees and I stopped to eat at a local restaurant. While we were dining, three uniformed soldiers and one guest walked in. I waited for a while to make sure they had all placed their orders. Then, without saying a word, I headed to the counter, where I could talk to their waitress. I informed her that I would like to take care of the entire check for the "military table." It was a very good feeling. I slipped back to my table without so much as a word to anyone. I am very appreciative of the efforts made by these young men and women to defend our country.

Robert
Blairsville, Pa.

To start off, Rose, I want you to scold our military people (yes, I said scold) for not wearing their uniforms out in public. I know there are more of them, and we hardly get to see any. As a result we don't have the chance to buy them gift cards or pay for their dinners—it's not fair! Whenever my husband and I go out to dinner we keep a sharp eye open for those in military uniform, and—whether it's in our budget or not—we buy. So please tell them over the radio to wear their uniforms more often so we can recognize them!

My story is a simple one. I had taken my brother to Columbus for a day; he had an appointment and he finds it difficult to drive long distances because he is partially disabled (due to a work injury). During the return trip we ate at a restaurant outside of Columbus. As we were finishing up dinner we noticed a woman and her eighteen-year-old son (he looked about that age, and his mom looked a little nervous); they sat down behind us. They were

joined by a man who shook their hands and mentioned that the young man had to sign a few papers.
I don't know what was said, but I suspected that this
young man was signing up for military service.

When I paid our bill I sent the waiter to find out
if that was the story. The waiter came back to tell me
that in fact the boy was signing up for one of the
services. I immediately told the waiter to ask them
what kind of pie or cake they wanted, and he
promptly did so; it was exciting to buy them a big
chocolate pie. I then left the restaurant, remaining
unknown to these people; I never allow waiters to
point me out—after all, it's not about me.

Still, I did get to see the young man diving into
the pie, and that made it all the more worth it. I say
a prayer for him when I remember this incident.
Hopefully, his mom also understands how many people are supporting the military and are praying for
them, and that may make her feel a little bit better
about letting her child go to fight for our freedoms.

Laura
Hiram, Ohio

I'm a trucker from Saxonburg, Pennsylvania, and I
was going to Zanesville, Ohio, from Ottawa, Illinois.
I was heading south on Interstate 65 and decided it
was time for supper at about 6:00 p.m. I pulled into

a truck stop that I knew had a good buffet, and once inside I sat down at a table beside a couple of soldiers. On my way to the buffet I went to the cashier and asked her to please take the soldiers' receipts and put them aside—I would pay for them when I paid my bill.

While I was eating, the soldiers went to pay their bill. I sat and watched as they were standing at the cashier and looking around the restaurant, trying to figure out who had bought their dinner. When I went to pay my bill the cashier almost had tears in her eyes when she told me that what I had done was the most unselfish thing she had seen in quite a while. I just said that it was the very least I could do, considering what they do for us.

Wesley
Saxonburg, Pa.

After church on Sunday my mother and I went to a Bob Evans restaurant in Greensburg, Pennsylvania. While waiting to be seated I noticed an older gentleman sitting with his wife and son, also waiting to be seated. He was wearing a D-Day Veteran pin. Needless to say, I was very impressed and couldn't believe I was standing near one of the soldiers from our country's greatest generation, let alone one who was on the beaches of Normandy.

I pointed out the man to my mom as we were being seated. While we continued eating, I noticed where the gentleman and his family were sitting. I then got the attention of their waitress and told her I would like to pick up their tab. I paid their bill but asked her not to reveal my identity to the soldier and to simply say, "Thank you for your service to our country. Your family's meal has been taken care of."

The veteran must have seen the waitress come to my table, because after his meal he came over and thanked us. While speaking with him he informed me that he completed five tours during World War II. It was only a short interaction, but one in which I felt privileged to take part. He and his family then left, and my mother and I finished our meal.

When we left to pay for our meal at the front desk the cashier asked if we were the ones who paid for the veteran's meal. I said, "Yes, why?" She then said, "Mike took care of your meal." I asked who Mike was, and she told me he was the manager and that our meal was on him today. It was a nice surprise. I was happy to cover the vet's meal, but the gesture put forth by the manager was truly unexpected.

It was great to see that the simple gesture of helping out a United States veteran affected him to extend the same kindness to a complete stranger. It was not my gesture that I felt was noteworthy—just something anyone would do knowing our country's history—but rather the action of the manager to extend his hand.

I just wanted you to know that not everyone takes for granted what made this country great, and many of us still believe in fighting to keep our nation free. It is a privilege to live in a free country but a responsibility to keep it so.

Jonathan
Greensburg, Pa.

It was an ordinary day in August in our household and we decided to take a ride to the Super Walmart in St. Mary's County, southern Maryland. On the way home, not far from where a country road merges into a four-lane highway, I started noticing people gathering along the way, holding flags and signs and wearing red, white, and blue clothing. A few miles up the highway I finally turned off the road and asked what was going on. It seems that groups of people from all walks of life, from proud vets and recently wounded soldiers to mothers holding their babies, were saying goodbye to one of our brave heroes, an Army sergeant who was killed in Afghanistan on August 1, 2008. He was twenty-four years old.

I didn't know the people who asked me to join

their group and I didn't have a flag or sign, but those things didn't matter. For the next hour we enjoyed each other's company, making small talk and trying to guess where the people in the passing cars were going—until a total silence fell upon our area of the highway and we heard the sirens. The procession to Arlington National Cemetery was approaching. As the procession passed we stood at attention with our hands over our hearts, each of us grateful that for once, instead of crying alone in our homes, we were able to gather together—to be physically present to honor the sergeant and his family, who gave so much for this country. You can call it luck, karma, or chance that I happened to be on that road on that date and time, but I choose to believe that God played a big part in my being there.

Alexandra
Southern Maryland

One evening my kids and I were grocery shopping in a local store when we happened to see a group of reservists shopping for supplies. I frantically rummaged through my purse looking for a gift card I thought I had. My plan was to let my seven-year-old daughter give it to the soldier of her choosing, but the card was nowhere to be found.

As I wallowed in my guilt for not being prepared and for not really being able to spare the extra cash, my heart pleaded with me to do the only thing I could do. I put aside my own guilt and approached a middle-aged soldier. "Excuse me," I said. "Yes, Ma'm," he replied. I was struck by his piercing ice-blue eyes. I proceeded to thank him and his fellow soldiers for all they do and told him that despite what they may hear in the mainstream media, they are truly loved and prayed for every night. Behind me, my daughter repeatedly chanted, "Thank you, Army man!"

As his eyes misted over, I felt the sting of fresh tears starting in my own. "You truly have no idea what this means to us, Ma'm. We thank *you*," he said. I told him to please stay safe and then let him continue his shopping.

Approaching the checkout with tears streaming down my face, my thirteen-year-old son (who is high-functioning autistic and had remained aloof during my conversation with the soldier) asked why I was crying. All I could say was that I had just had a short conversation with an angel sent by God to protect us. I explained that not everyone feels selfless enough to volunteer to make the ultimate sacrifice, and that those who do are angels.

"What did you say, Mom?" my son asked. I told him about my conversation and that he should not be afraid to thank those who defend our freedom and protect us from evil.

"That's a relief, Mom," he replied. "I thought maybe you were asking if he knew of a good military school to send me to because I haven't always been good to my sister." Needless to say, my tears of admiration were mixed with tears of laughter.

This was an experience I know will remain with me forever. I've also learned to be prepared for my next meeting with an angel.

Denise
Champion, Pa.

For the past three years our family has hosted a very casual get-together to help make teenagers aware that there are many young men and women fighting overseas for their freedom.

It started when I learned that a friend's daughter was marrying a soldier who was being deployed to Iraq. I was so consumed by his story that I wanted the teenage friends of my daughters here in Peters Township to understand what was going on in the world outside their bubble and to take a few minutes to write letters expressing their gratitude.

In the past, I always had a neighborhood Halloween driveway party, so I just converted that effort to a "neighborhood" writing-to-a-soldier party; I invited everyone to come over to have hot chocolate and homemade stromboli and to sit down and write a letter. I try to schedule this event during the first week of December—which is a nice time because it is right after Thanksgiving and before the hectic holiday season. I supply the writing paper, stamped envelopes, and pens and spread them around my big dining-room table. It is a beautiful sight, watching the teens thoughtfully writing to soldiers not that much older than they are. Most of the soldiers we write to are from the annual list that our local newspaper distributes around Thanksgiving. I provide those names and also encourage neighbors and friends to bring their personal lists.

The adults who participated were very grateful for the opportunity to write letters. Everyone loved the fact that there was an easy forum through which to extend thanks to those serving our country.

In the first year, we asked the invitees not only write a letter but also to bring small items to send out. The response was overwhelming, and we ended up shipping about fifteen boxes of goods. We have since settled in to just writing nice letters—and trying to make these simple acts of kindness an annual tradition in our household, hosted by myself, my husband, and our two daughters.

Trish
Peters Township, Pa.

Honor is a hard term to describe. It doesn't have a color or weight or shape. If someone were to ask me what honor looked like, I'd probably struggle with what to say.

But something happened on May 23, 2012, at 9:31 a.m. at Gate 38 of Reagan National Airport that might change that. A flash mob of sorts broke out. But not like you've seen on YouTube, with highly choreographed dance numbers or people singing a song in unison. In fact, virtually all of the participants of this "flash mob" didn't know they would be participating until moments before it happened.

Let me explain. Shortly before 9:30 over the loudspeakers a US Airways gate attendant announced that an Honor Flight of World War II veterans would be arriving momentarily and encouraged anyone passing by to help greet them. Five or six people looked like they were officially part of the welcoming committee, and the rest of the people in the secure section of the airport were regular old travelers going somewhere. Then I had a terrible thought: What if these veterans came off the plane and just those five or six individuals were there to greet them? I walked a gate over to help see the veterans out.

But then it happened—and frankly, I wasn't

expecting it. All throughout the terminal, people left their gates and gathered around Gate 38. A few active military personnel in plain clothes approached the gate attendant and politely asked if they could join in the salute within the jetway as the heroes first stepped off the plane. Every human being in the terminal stood at attention and faced the door.

Someone held up an old newspaper from 1945 that had a banner headline reading "Nazis Quit"—and when I saw that newspaper, I realized that World War II wasn't just a chapter in a history book. It was men and women who saw an evil like the world has never seen before and traveled across the world to meet that evil. And they defeated it.

I wonder if in 1945, any of those brave soldiers could ever imagine that 67 years later we'd still be basking in the freedom that they preserved. And some of those heroes were about to walk through Gate 38.

The first soldier walked through the door. Old, frail, and needing help walking. And every person I could see in the entire airport stood and applauded. No, maybe cheered is more like it.

But here's the thing—the applause didn't stop. For a full 20 minutes, as veteran by veteran stepped out of the jetway, the US Airways wing of Reagan National Airport thundered in appreciation. Travelers stepped out for the opportunity to shake their hands while others held back tears.

This is the America we picture in our heads. Heroes getting a hero's welcome and those who enjoy the freedom adequately conveying their gratitude.

Now I know what honor looks like.

Chris
"What Honor Looks Like" from his website,
www.mullerover.com

3
Proud Families

We live in Rockingham, North Carolina, very close to Fort Bragg, and we frequently see soldiers out and about (Army, unlike Marines, can wear their cammies off base). I've often paid restaurant tabs and even grocery bills!

Here's one particularly heart-warming story. My husband is a Marine (not active, but once a Marine, always a Marine), and when he and my eighty-two-year-old uncle, a World War II Pacific Theater Marine, get together, it's on! The jarhead still comes out in my uncle. He's a very spry eighty-two. Last year for St. Patrick's Day he came to visit and we went to the beach. He wanted to celebrate St. Patty's Day at a Margaritaville restaurant.

Sitting next to us at the bar were several "new" Marines on leave from Camp Lejeune. When they heard Uncle Marvin was a World War II vet (I will tell everyone who will listen), they were all over him, shaking his hand, taking their pictures with him, and thanking him for his service and "setting the standard they hoped to live up to." What wonderful young men. It still brings tears to my eyes!

Charlita
Rockingham, N.C.

Our son, Stephen, age nineteen, returned home from six months of Air Force basic and technical training this past Friday.

He was a little nervous about wearing his "camo gear" in the airports—he didn't want to stick out or get stares from people. I told him not to worry—the public is generally appreciative of our military men and women, and I was proven right. Stevie said that a woman in the airport came up and thanked him for his service, and on one of his flights a gentleman sitting in first class insisted that Stevie take his seat. It turned out this very nice man was retired Air Force and he knew exactly what our son had just been through.

Karen and Steve
Duncansville, Pa.

My son just returned from Iraq, where he was stationed at a forward operations base near Ramadie.

He asked if I would go with him to purchase a car to drive back to Camp Lejeune, North Carolina.

We bought the vehicle at a local dealership and were waiting for the final paperwork. An elderly gentleman walked by and greeted us. I need to mention that Marines do not wear their camo off base, so nobody would know that they are members of our armed services (apart from the jarhead haircut).

The man asked what we were up to, so I mentioned that my son just returned from Iraq and we were purchasing a car. The man looked at my son, reached into his pocket, and handed him a fifty-dollar bill. My son declined, saying that it wasn't necessary; but the man insisted, saying, "Have dinner on me."

My son took the money with a big grin on his face. He hadn't realized how supportive of our troops people are.

Anyway, I later found out that the man was the owner of the dealership. Needless to say, that will be the first place I stop when looking for a new car.

Kent
Venetia, Pa.

My father was a Marine in World War II and served aboard the USS *Vincennes*, which was sunk during

the battle of Savo Island in the Guadalcanal campaign. He survived to have five children. My oldest
brother was also a Marine, and my second brother
was a Seabee, as is my brother-in-law. These three
served during the Vietnam War. My oldest brother,
Andrew, was "extended" during his enlistment, to be
sent to Vietnam during the early years. He was stationed at Phu Bai near Hue, the DMZ.

Andy enlisted at seventeen; therefore, he was
about twenty-one when he was there, around 1965.
This was a time when supplies were so limited that
he recalls getting off the truck, reporting to his sergeant and asking to be issued a weapon, and then
having been offered a sidearm that the sergeant possessed or a sawed-off shotgun. Nevertheless, having
been radio trained, he was assigned to regular recon
duty. He was involved in much direct action with the
enemy.

After our mother died I was bringing some
items to his home in New Jersey and noticed that on
the wall was a display box of his medals, including a
Purple Heart and service ribbons he obtained while
attached to the USMC. Inside this box was a gleaming
red-and-yellow-ribboned medal with a small star inside a large star. I looked at my brother and said,
"Andy, that's a Silver Star! That's the second highest
award we give for bravery in this country." He
replied, "No, it's not. It's the third highest." I re-
sponded, "That doesn't matter. My brother is a war

hero and nobody knows about it? We put guys like you in front of parades!"

Andy stood silent, not addressing my comments. I made sure I called my sisters and other brothers to tell them of this previously hidden honor.

There is a postscript to this story. A box brought from my mother's home contained a simple envelope from the Department of the Navy. It had never been opened and was in a stack of mail from thirty years earlier that my mother had collected to save for Andrew while he was overseas. This envelope contained the notice of his original citation of gallantry and award of the Silver Star. My parents died without knowing how brave he was. My brother is a real hero, and I am so very proud of him.

Anthony
Hopewell Junction, N.Y.

My husband, Paul, is a flight surgeon in the Pennsylvania National Guard. He was on his way to San Antonio for a military conference this past Monday, so he was in full uniform. During his layover in Dallas, he stopped for a steak dinner at a restaurant in the airport. After enjoying his meal, he found out that the bill had been paid by someone who wanted to remain anonymous.

I can only imagine how Paul felt. I can tell you that it warmed my heart that he is cared for by anonymous angels on this earth. He will be deploying to Iraq this year, and things like this just make me feel better.

Ellen
Belle Vernon, Pa.

Rose, I wanted to tell you about an experience I had a few months back that still brings tears to my eyes every time I think about it.

I have a son in the Navy. He has just completed his ninth year. I also have a stepson in the Air Force who is serving on his fifth tour in Iraq and is planning on re-enlisting while over there. I could not be more proud.

My husband and I have made it a practice to pay the bills for our servicemen and servicewomen whenever we are out and they are in the restaurant. We do it anonymously and just inform the waitress to tell them that we appreciate their service.

My daughter and I were having lunch at T.G.I. Friday's when six airmen came in for lunch. I went to the back and told the waitress to give me their bill.

While we were waiting, one airman got a call that four more were joining them, so they asked to be moved to a larger table in another section. The same waitress would wait on them and she asked me if I still wanted to pay, as there would now be ten. I told her yes!

When my daughter and I were finished eating, the waitress brought me all the bills. My daughter went to the restroom while I waited for her at my table. When the waitress returned she handed me a patch that read "758th Airlift Squadron" and told me that the airman said thank you and wanted the person who paid for his group's lunches to have this patch.

Of course I immediately got all choked up. As I waited for my daughter I saw an airman go to the back of the restaurant and talk to the waitress. He obviously asked who paid, since he headed right for me. He said thank you and wanted to know if he could buy us drinks or dessert or anything. I thanked him and told him he was already doing more than I could ever want. As we were talking, I told him about my sons and said I didn't know who had given me the patch but I was deeply honored. Soon a second airman came by, so I also explained to him that an airman had given me his patch, which I showed him, saying how much I would treasure it. That airman looked over his uniform and pulled a patch reading "Air Force Reserve Command" right off his sleeve.

I could hardly talk—I was so touched by these men. I was just trying to make their day a pleasant one by buying them lunch. In giving me those patches they have touched my life forever.

I am truly grateful for the men and women of our military and will continue to buy meals for as many as possible. I also have heard you suggest giving them gift cards, and I am starting to do that as well.

Gaylind
Burgettstown, Pa.

My son Daniel is in the Air Force and works with the Security Forces. He has been deployed to Saudi Arabia, Korea, Iraq, and Kyrgyzstan. His six-year enlistment is up in two weeks and our family will be glad to have him home.

One of the many jobs of the Security Forces is to guard the aircraft that deliver supplies to enemy zones. They are the first to jump out of a plane and set up a secure perimeter so that the supply crew can unload the cargo in safety. They are one of the groups that are never heard about yet are necessary to the entire war effort.

When Daniel came home on leave during his

tour in Iraq, I flew down to Robins Air Force Base in Georgia to meet him and bring him home for several weeks. Our flight from Atlanta to Pittsburgh was un-eventful except for one thing. A stewardess came by and questioned Daniel about his branch of service—where he had been, how long he was home, etc. A little while later she came back and told him that it was both an honor and a pleasure to have him on the flight and then asked that we please accompany her up to first class! Additionally, she got on the inter-com and told all the passengers about Daniel's story. The passengers then gave him a round of applause. It was a wonderful gesture.

Tracy
Eldersville, Pa.

I live in the Dallas, Texas, area, where we get a lot of soldiers passing through. My wife's nephew, Chris, of Burley, Idaho, was one of those soldiers. He called late one weekday night and said that he was en route from Iraq to Idaho and that he would have a half-day's layover in Dallas and would like to see the family if possible.

My wife and three teenage daughters met him at 5:30 a.m. in the lobby of the hotel, where he had slept for a couple of hours. Christopher told of his travel adventures, which included a long delay in a European airport, where he had lost his backpack and all of its contents—an iPod and tennis shoes; gifts for his mom, girlfriend, and six siblings; plus assorted snacks.

They went to a Denny's restaurant for breakfast and caught up on family news. When it was time to leave, Christopher wanted to pay for the breakfast, but the waitress said that it was already taken care of, including the tip. No one took credit for the event. The Denny's manager thanked him for his service and made sure that the staff assembled to wave as they left the restaurant.

My wife then took him shopping for replacement gifts and shoes. At every turn he was treated like a celebrity—people shaking his hand, asking for a picture with him, and thanking him for his service.

At lunch the same thing happened. The check never arrived and the waitress would not accept any money. The staff there also waved and thanked him as they left. My wife called to let me know how touched they were by the events of that morning and the kindness of the people here in Dallas toward Chris. She could not hold back the tears.

We have put off writing you to share these events, since neither one of us can think of this wonderful experience without tearing up to the point of not being able to read the computer screen. I do want to let your audience know how good the people are in our country.

Gregg
Dallas, Tex.

My brother, Ryan, had been serving in Iraq since December 25, 2007, when we were told he would be coming home on leave for five days in late March of 2008. Ryan is a huge Pittsburgh Penguins hockey fan and he told me that one of the top things he wanted to do when he came home was to attend a hockey game. The Penguins had only one home game during his leave, which was scheduled for March 31, 2008. I wanted to purchase four tickets so that we could go as a family. However, due to the success of the Penguins, there had been forty-one consecutive sell-outs. I really wanted to purchase these tickets for Ryan so that he could enjoy a hockey game during his brief leave.

I had e-mailed your radio program, Rose, inquiring if anyone known to you had tickets to this game and if that person would be willing to sell them to us at face value. Two weeks later, with only about ten days before the game, *America's Morning Show with Quinn and Rose* aired our request live. The response was overwhelming! Not only did a local man call in and donate four tickets at no cost to us, but we also got donations for four dinners to Outback Steakhouse, one donation of $100 cash to use for concessions and parking at the game, a cash donation of $150 for dinner at a place of our choice, and a $50 gift card to Dick's Sporting Goods; plus, a local photographer donated his time to join us at the game and take pictures of us.

My original modest request directed to your the radio show resulted in four donated tickets, along with cash and gift certificates galore. I was speechless when your producer called to get my address and all the information necessary to forward the donations to me for my brother's leave. Additionally, with only two days left before the game, a business associate of my father donated six tickets to the same game, allowing us to host the photographer along with some friends and family members.

When Ryan called home to talk to my father shortly before beginning his leave, he was told about the numerous donations and all he could do was whisper a soft "thank you" on the other end of the phone line. He truly was speechless over the generosity shown by complete strangers, all simply due to a request on the radio.

The goodness in people is not always evident in Ryan's line of work, but it surely was shown to him on this day. Because of the wonderful donations we were able to have an enjoyable evening of fun that we will all remember for a lifetime. Thank you, everyone who made this possible.

Michael
Southwestern Pa.

Rose, I am a recently remarried U.S. Navy widow and listen to your show whenever my schedule permits (which isn't nearly often enough). I was listening today when you interviewed Ryan regarding the donations that other listeners gave him as thanks for his service. I wanted to take the time to also thank your listeners for doing that. I try to pay for meals anonymously whenever I see a military person because I have found that I still cannot verbally thank them for the service that they and their families provide for our continued freedom without unintentionally crying—even almost six years after the death of my husband. I loved being a military wife and the hardest thing that I have ever done was to learn to live as a "regular" civilian.

At the time of the military-training-plane collision that took the lives of my lieutenant husband Chris and six other aviators on May 8, 2002, my two children were only about six months old and two years old. Luckily the Holy Spirit inspired me to ask for memory letters so that my children could learn about their father as they grew up. I now have a two-inch binder filled with letters, short and long, from people who knew him in high school, college, and the military. I even received some from people who met him just once or who saw him only at church or out running on the road. Some of the letters that mean the most to me are short, simple statements. I have copied all the letters and made a duplicate book for my late husband's parents and siblings; they will be able to read these stories about their son/brother whenever they need to be reminded— especially by those who served with him—that his death was not in vain. One military aviator even had his father stop at Arlington Cemetery and take pictures and a paper rubbing of Chris's memorial stone to be included in the book.

There are three examples from the memorial book that I wanted to share with you.

Three months after Chris died I received a card from a brigadier general. I have never met the man and I am assuming that he must have met my husband when he served as the junior executive officer to the Director of Intelligence at STRATCOM at Offutt Air Force Base in Bellevue, Nebraska. He simply wrote to my children, "I'd like to tell you something about your dad. He was a man with sparkling eyes, a great sense of adventure, and much mischief. My own dad died just last week. The highest praise that I can give your father is that, in many, many ways, he reminded me of my own. I hope—and I know—that you will live your lives in ways that will make him proud." My husband died at the age of twenty-six. I am grateful that anyone, especially a brigadier general, would take the time while dealing with his own grief to tell my children that their father reminded him of his own dad. I still tear up just thinking about it.

The second example came from a young aviator, whom I ran into a few times after Chris died. Every time I saw him I asked him for a memory letter, even though he only knew my husband for a few short months. (I was obsessed over the memory book—I knew that the children would have many, many questions about Chris, since they wouldn't have any memories of their own.) More than a year later the aviator finally sent me a letter. He wrote about a dinner that he had with Chris in Key West, Florida, two months before my husband's death. They were dining out; possibly there had been some drinking going on, and the group must have started telling "women stories." The aviator reported that my husband simply said, "My wife is my best friend." The aviator said that those words stopped him in his tracks. He has often thought of what Chris said, and he hopes that someday he will have that type of relationship with his future wife. While I knew in my heart that we were "best friends," it was so wonderful to hear that my husband had verbally testified to that! The letter also came on a day when I was in desperate need of being reminded of Chris's love because I was still so lonely—especially late at night and on weekends, when all my friends were busy with their own families.

The third example occurred when I remarried several years later. One of my wedding presents came in the form of a memory letter—years after Chris had died! The wife of that aviator had been hounding her husband off and on for all those years to mail me the letter. I guess he had typed it right after Chris died but wanted to "rewrite" it by hand so that it would be more personal. His wife finally made him print it from the computer, and she included it with the present that she had bought for us. His letter meant more to me than the other wedding present they sent.

I would like everyone to know that it is never too late to send someone stories and memories of their departed loved one! You never "move on" after the death of someone you love—you simply learn how to continue living with the loss. Also, your listeners should know that it is statistically proven that only widows/widowers who were happily married to begin with will remarry after the death of their spouse. (People need to be careful when passing judgment regarding someone beginning to date again or getting remarried after the death of a spouse.)

I am fortunate enough to now be married to a former Army reservist who realizes that the children, who are now about six and eight, need to know about their biological father, who is in heaven—and also about all the men and women who served with him in the war on terrorism. They also need to know that we must win this war and fight for the American way of life. Shortly after Chris died, I made the decision that I was not going to allow his death to be the biggest event in our lives—we were never going to make excuses. We can best honor Chris by choosing to be happy and living our lives to give glory to God.

I will not allow Chris's death to be in vain, and so I try to support our military in any way I can. I take my children to the Memorial Day and Veteran's Day services. They are now old enough to understand why I often pay for service members' meals. I try to live a life of service in other ways, such as volunteering to coach soccer and catechesis. The greatest compliment that someone once gave me was when another soccer mom stopped me a year after I moved to Steubenville, Ohio, and said, "You must be a good mother, because your children are always smiling whenever I see them." I can testify that God is the provider for all widows and the fatherless or motherless children of the world, and that His grace alone will slowly get you through those trials in life that you think you simply cannot bear!

Stephanie
Steubenville, Ohio

Well, my son went back to Iraq this morning. It was so good to see him for a few weeks. He might be home by December! When my husband took Jack to the airport, a security guard stopped them and asked where my son was going. He said he was returning to Iraq. The security guard said, "Military doesn't wait in line when I'm on duty"—and he walked my son past the forty-minute line to the front! This is a great "thanking a soldier" story because it's these little things that make you feel good.

Linda
Pittsburgh, Pa.

My brother-in-law is a captain in the Army, stationed at Fort Riley in Kansas. He and my sister were married in June 2006, and he left the following February for a fifteen-month tour of duty in Iraq. When he left, my husband and I talked at length to our daughter, Sophia, about where her uncle was going and why. We made sure to put together care packages for him every month and lit candles for his safety every Sunday in church. My husband, who puts her to bed, says that she prayed for him faithfully every night.

My sister being married to a soldier really illustrated for us the sacrifice that all of these men and women make. So, whenever we would see military personnel, Sophia and I would thank them for their service and tell them about her uncle. One day we were at a local mall and happened to see a man in his fatigues. I didn't have much cash on me, so I quickly grabbed two five-dollar bills and gave them to Sophia, instructing her to give them to the Army guy; I told her to thank him and explain that lunch was on us. She tore off down the mall and handed him the money and said, "Here—thank you!" He looked at me, confused, and when I said we wanted to buy him lunch, he replied that he couldn't take the money. That's when my daughter said that her uncle was in Iraq. He just looked at me and said "I'd feel bad ..." So I told him that the least we could do for him was pay for his meal. He took the money, reluctantly, and thanked us. My daughter skipped along, happy at what she had done. When she asked me why we did that, I told her because that could be her uncle in a mall, or airport, or anywhere, and I'd hope that someone would do the same for him.

I am so grateful for what you do, Rose, by passing along your soldier stories. I think people don't understand how much they mean to the members of the military, and also to their spouses and families who give up so much when they are left behind as their loved ones go off to war. My sister often said it made things easier for her to know that so many people supported what her husband was doing.

Jenny
Mt. Lebanon, Pa.

My son was in the Marine Corps for four years and did two tours in Afghanistan immediately following 9/11. When he came home from his first tour, he was overwhelmed with support and thanks from the community. After the second tour, the tone in the United States had started to shift and the support had slipped.

On Veteran's Day this year, I was in a restaurant in Lancaster, Ohio, and noticed a young soldier sitting with a woman I assumed was his mom. I asked the server to quietly give me his bill so I could anonymously pay tribute to him. However, the server told the young soldier who was paying the bill, and he and his mom came to my table. The mother was crying and he looked surprised. I started to weep myself as I told them how much respect I had for young people who volunteer to serve their country. He and his mom both hugged me. It was so moving, for all of us.

At this time in our history, it is even more important to honor these men and women. They are starting to feel negative vibes form the press and college students. We must continue to make these young people aware of our support in any way we can.

Barbara
Columbus, Ohio

My daughter, Cheryl, and her fiancé, Joe, took their care packages to the post office in mid-December to mail them to my wife's brother, Michael, and his unit in northern Iraq. They explained to the postal worker how many they had and needed to send them to Iraq, and the woman was happy to help. As they were working to process the boxes, a line formed at the counter and that postal worker had to take care of the new customers. By the time she was done with everyone else it was closing time. Cheryl said they would come back another time to finish. But the woman offered to stay and take care of them—they worked for almost another hour to get all the packages done.

On January 1, Michael called from Iraq and said the boxes got there on Christmas Eve and the guys were thrilled with the treats and small games they got. The care packages were funded in part from donations that came from members of a Lutheran church in Somerset, Pennsylvania, where my wife, Michelle, my son, Anthony, and Cheryl are members.

May God bless all our military personnel and their families.

Mark
Somerset, Pa.

While our son, who had spent the past fifteen months in Iraq, was on his way home for his midtour leave, the plane was routed through Atlanta. All on board were military coming home on leave. The pilot called ahead and they announced in Atlanta's airport that this plane was landing with soldiers aboard.

As the solders disembarked they were met by a huge, cheering crowd. My son said the people wanted to talk to all of them and were so enthusiastic that some of the soldiers almost missed their connecting flights.

My son has also told me that he purposely does not wear his uniform since so many people buy him things when he does. He feels it is just part of his job and duty and does not expect gifts.

He has also told us many positive things about his tour. I wish more people were able to hear about the good things that occur in the middle of such a war zone. I feel that the young children whose lives have changed because of our soldiers will one day bring about a new Iraq.

Linda
Washington, Pa.

I work from home over the Internet, and as a consequence I chat with a number of people online. I "met" a woman from the Philly area online. A divorced mom, her oldest son was in Iraq in the First Armored Division. I quickly became friends with Cheri and even chatted online with her son, Justin, while he was in Iraq. Cheri was so stressed out by the war that she unplugged the TV. Most of the news coverage was negative, and for her as a mother it was evidently too much to take.

Justin was doing well, calling home often, but in a war zone things happen fast. The first time Justin was wounded, he was hit by some shrapnel, but the wounds were minor. He called home to tell Cheri, "Hey, Mom, guess what? I got wounded." He knew it was minor, but no war wound is minor to a mother. Poor Justin just didn't realize what he was putting his mom through. Justin got wounded a second time by more shrapnel, and the second wound was serious enough not to make a call home about it—although thankfully not so serious that it would cause lasting damage. Justin was in the lead tank, and his actions got him recommended for the Bronze Star.

Sometime later, on patrol, Justin was shot by a sniper. The bullet passed through his butt and came out of his thigh, narrowly missing the bone—but the wound was grievous enough. For weeks and months in the hospital, first at Ramstein Air Base and later at Walter Reed, Justin fought to keep his leg. Were it not for his mother's effort, demanding the level of care he needed, it is doubtful Justin would have recovered. Justin is out of the Army now. His leg is not totally healed—nor will it probably ever completely heal; but he has use of it and for that he is thankful.

I have never met Justin or his mother. I have only talked to them a handful of times. I was so moved by the sacrifices made by this family, I felt obliged to show them some kind of gratitude. I sent Justin a gift certificate to Ruth's Chris Steak House sufficiently funded to feed his family. Justin wanted me to join them, but I declined—because if I had, it would then be about me. It's not about me. It's about Justin and Cheri and those thousands and thousands of families who join our beloved military. It is about the willingness to take on the job of defending this country with one's life. I honor their willingness and I honor their commitment. I work from my home in comfort, enjoying the fruits of freedom, grown from a soil made fertile by the blood of patriots like Justin and Cheri, and many thousands of others. God bless them all and God bless our great country and our precious freedoms.

Anthony
Carmel, N.Y.

A few years ago in August my eighteen-year-old son joined the National Guard. After his Guard weekend in January, my son and two of his fellow Guard members went out to a local pizza restaurant. In the booth next to them there was a young mother and her small daughter (about six years old). The woman did not speak to them in the restaurant, but when they left and went to their respective cars, she went to my son's car. When he rolled down his window, she told him that she just wanted to thank him for the service the three of them were giving our country.

She then handed him three gift cards. My son thanked her and told her she didn't have to do that, but she insisted. The gift cards were from two major chain department stores. My son, without looking at their value, handed his friends cards and repeated what the woman had said. After he got home and told me this story, I looked at his card and on the back was an amount of $150! He then sent text messages to his friends, and theirs were worth $75 each.

Apparently, this young mother, not knowing beforehand that the three Guard soldiers would be in the restaurant, must have given them her own gift cards that she (or her daughter) received as Christmas gifts. How great to provide her daughter with such a wonderful lesson in appreciation and generosity.

Donna
Butler, Pa.

Rose, I heard your radio broadcast with the story about the lady who insisted on trading seats with the soldier on a recent airline flight. It is heartwarming to know that there are still people out there that appreciate our guys and gals serving their country. In fact, this is probably the majority of our population, although you will not hear that from most media.

My son is in the Ohio National Guard. Several years ago, he retuned from Kosovo after a year-long "UN Peacekeeping" mission. Their overseas aircraft landed in New Hampshire about 2:00 a.m. for refueling. The soldiers were met by a local chapter of the VFW, and they had brought along handshakes, doughnuts, and coffee. These guys made it a point to meet that aircraft at 2:00 a.m.! Our guys were really stunned by their kindness.

Rick
Canal Fulton, Ohio

My son returned from Baghdad last month for a visit and he said a lot of people came up to him and thanked him for his service. The area in Iraq that they controlled had just three businesses open when they got there, and now there are more than five hundred businesses and it is going well.

Jerry
Strasburg, Ohio

My son, who serves in the Pennsylvania Army National Guard, is currently attending Kutztown University of Pennsylvania and coming home once a month for weekend drills with his unit in Indiana, Pennsylvania.

This past Monday, before Matt returned to school, his mom, her sister, and I took him out to dinner at a local restaurant. Before we ordered our meals, the waiter asked if we would like anything from the bar, since one of the other patrons was offering to buy our party drinks. The restaurant was not crowded, so we were able to determine that the offer was made by a young couple; they are neighbors and friends of ours. None of us was able to accept their offer of drinks because we all had things to do after dinner, but we waived and told them we'd take a rain check.

After dinner, the couple came over to our table and we talked for quite a while; it had been several months since either of them had seen Matt. When I was ready to leave, I flagged down the waiter to get my check, but he said our meals had already been paid for. By the time I turned around, our two neighbors were headed for the door with big smiles on their faces. When I told my son what they had done, he informed me that the same kind of thing has been happening to him for the past year or so.

Randy
Indiana County, Pa.

My son Matthew, a second lieutenant in the U. S. Army, is currently attending Ranger School. He was a West Point graduate in May 2011. He had prior service before attending West Point, which included a Purple Heart and lots of other ribbons he wore on his uniform while a cadet.

One year he and a few other cadets were invited to attend a cotillion ball in New York over the Christmas holidays and they were dressed in their military whites, which are quite impressive. After dancing for a while he came back to his table and found a velvet box sitting on his plate. Under the box was a note that read "Thank you for your service," and inside the box was a brand new Rolex watch! He looked around and no one could (or would) tell him who had left it for him. Ever since he told me this story I have felt amazed and grateful to all the generous and patriotic people in this country. And I am proud to be an American mom of a potential American Army Ranger!

Michelle
North Monmouth, Maine

4
Our Troops and Vets in Their Own Words

Rose, I have been listening to your show for quite a while now. I have also been an active-duty soldier in the Army for the last nineteen years. I chose this life and career for many reasons, not the least of which was to protect what I believe in and love: the United States.

On a personal level, I have always been somewhat embarrassed when people approach me and thank me for my service. I have always thought, "Why should they thank me for doing what I feel is my obligation and duty?" I have also frequently felt the venom on the other side of the coin, which unfortunately also occurs today.

Your efforts are quite appreciated and have endeared you to many a service member. That being said, I have often thought of what I could do to repay "you civilians" for the kindness being shown us. The answer struck me a few days ago while eating lunch in a restaurant. There were two elderly ladies in the booth across from me and I thought of all the stories you read on the air. So I picked up their tab and walked out.

Thank you for what you do. It is appreciated more than you know.

Thomas (Sgt., First Class, U.S. Army)

When I travel I usually use my military ID, as I hope it helps put people a little at ease in that I'm retired military. In the last couple of years I've had most airline employees and Transport Security Administration employees thank me for my service. Very heartwarming for me, especially since I'm from the Berkeley, California, area, where the sentiment isn't shared.

My service is one of the things I'm very proud of, and I'm sensitive to anyone who criticizes our outstanding military. I make it a point to talk to those in uniform and let them know that I'm retired military and how much I appreciate their service—and I tell them how much service meant to me personally. Along with that, quite frankly I had the time of my life during my military career, even though there were low points with the loss of friends over the years. If someone had told me when I was eighteen that I'd go on to fly the F-14 for most of my adult life,

I would have thought they were smoking something funny (a very real possibility in Berkeley).

Dave (Cdr. [Ret.], U.S. Navy)

My husband and I are both Army reservists (more than twenty years each), currently activated at bases in Texas. My Reserve unit was conducting its two-week annual training in San Pedro, California. We were a little worried about the reaction we would get running around southern California in our Army uniforms but were pleasantly surprised at the number of people who came up to us and thanked us for our service. Toward the end of the two weeks, our battalion commander held a "staff meeting" for about ten of us at Marie Callender's restaurant in nearby Rancho Palos Verdes. This was in a very nice shopping complex, and we certainly stood out in our uniforms.

We ate lunch, and as we finished, the waitress told us that dessert was on an unidentified gentleman who insisted on buying for us. We hadn't planned on dessert but didn't want to make the man feel slighted, so we each got something. After that, the waitress brought the bills to us but came back less than a minute later, saying there was a mistake, and she collected all the checks. When she returned she said that someone had picked up the entire bill. On top of that, the staff had more offers to buy our meals than there were opportunities! We were so appreciative! When we walked out of the restaurant, everyone inside clapped as we walked by. I kept the tears from flowing until I left the restaurant.

Cheryn (Maj., BDE S1, Hood MOB Brigade,
U.S. Army)

I heard Rose read the item about the aged/dying Marine who was visited by a Marine recruiter, whose only offer was to give him the smartest salute-in-dress-blues he could. Here is a related tale of my own.

At Thanksgiving last year, my father-in-law from Chicago came to visit us here in Beaver County, Pennsylvania. He asked to take a day trip to D.C. so he could see the World War II Memorial. He's in his eighties and was eighteen years old when he enlisted in 1941. He was Navy, Pacific Fleet, radioman, saw action many times, and was sunk twice. He was once temporarily blinded after being sunk, due to swimming in a fuel spill.

So we drove Friday morning and got there about noon. After parking, we walked to the Mall, where we spent quite a while at the Memorial. It turns out that my father-in-law has a lot of interesting stories that no one in the family had previously heard. Until his wife passed away in 2001, he never wanted to talk about the war much. Once she was gone, he opened up.

We left the World War II Memorial and headed off to other sites like the Vietnam Memorial. In early afternoon, we left him and our daughter on a bench while my wife and I went to one of those overpriced sandwich shacks nearby. They were selling kitsch along with sandwiches, including ball caps. We got him a navy-blue cap that read "World War II Veteran"—nothing fancy, really. We brought it back with the sandwiches and drinks and he thanked us for it and put it on. After we finished lunch, we considered heading for the Lincoln Memorial.

We almost never got there. From the time we stood up from the bench to start toward the other sites, my father-in-law could hardly walk fifty feet with that cap on his head without some random stranger stepping up to introduce himself, shake his hand, and thank him for his service. It was amazing and totally unexpected. He was all smiles and very good-natured about it. A few of the well-wishers were similarly aged gents who briefly shared details of where they had served and under what command.

We decided to stay through Saturday so we could visit Arlington Cemetery. My father-in-law wore his cap that day, too, and again he was frequently stopped for thank yous. We took the tram to get around Arlington. After realizing his vet status, the tram guide with the microphone started off the tour by announcing: "Ladies and gentlemen, we are proud to say that we have an actual World War II vet with us today." More than fifty people gave him a standing ovation.

Acquiring the cap was just an impulse buy, but we thought it would be nice to tell the nearby world about his vet status while we were visiting these sites. We weren't expecting so many people to show that kind of respect for a vet nor that it would impart so much enjoyment and pride to my father-in-law.

What a great way to let an old vet bask in some well-deserved glory!

Finally, here are a few of his recently revealed war stories. He had a regular horseshoe-throwing date with Admiral Nimitz and a couple of captains while he was on Okinawa—just a lowly radioman, regularly rubbing elbows with the brass. We also learned that he was at the raising of the flag on Iwo Jima. No, he wasn't one of the famous group of men who are known for raising it. But I learned from him (later confirmed by research) that, in fact, there were two flag raisings on Iwo Jima.

Karl
Beaver County, Pa.

For my son Henry's eighth birthday, we had a swim party for the boys in his second-grade class. Instead of presents, we asked everyone to bring items to donate to the troops. I included in the invitations a list of items the troops seem to always request. All the parents thought this was a great idea and were very supportive. We collected enough items to fill five boxes, which we shipped to several different addresses in the Middle East.

We later received a nice letter from John, a sergeant in Iraq. He included several pictures of his fellow soldiers, his barracks, and even a camel. We sent the letter and pictures to school for my son's teacher to read to the class and to post for all to see. From what the teacher and my son told me, his letter was very well received.

This was a great project for our family. Believe it or not, my son didn't even miss getting birthday presents!

Coleen
Gibsonia, Pa.

I was in a restaurant with my ex-wife—we were on our way home to pick up my son from his baby sitter, so we stopped for lunch. After we finished eating, we asked for the check, but the waitress informed us that a couple had already paid our bill. We asked who they were so we could personally thank them.

The waitress informed us that they had already left. I was very thankful—especially when contemplating how nice someone can be without wanting any gratitude in return. I'd say I wish more people were like this—but in reality they are, at least in my experience.

Sean (Sgt., Training NCO, U.S. Army)

Rose, I heard you relating a few stories of kind acts by people toward service members in uniform and had to tell you my story from a different time.

I was commissioned a lieutenant in 1986 and reported to Maintenance Management Officers Basic Course of the Ordnance Center and School at Aberdeen Proving Ground, Maryland. I landed at Baltimore/Washington airport on a sweltering June Tuesday with all but fifty dollars of my self-worth invested in my required uniforms (officers buy their own and pay their own way despite appearances), which neatly fit into two duffel bags. I looked for the shuttle bus (which my paperwork described) outside the luggage area and discovered some bad news—shuttles only run on weekends.

The information desk was helpful in defining my options, but my remaining cash had to provide more than taxi service to the base. Since I couldn't afford any of the available means to get me to Aberdeen, I left the terminal in uniform with a duffel bag on each shoulder, and headed to the north on foot. I imagined I could get to the parkway and be among enough service members in the traffic that I could catch a ride. It didn't take long to both break a huge sweat in the dark green and to hear a hailing call from the long-term-parking rows.

A fellow passenger on my connection from Atlanta, on his way home to Edgewood, Maryland (just south of Aberdeen), recognized that I needed a ride and that I might have the stuff to figure out why his car wouldn't start. It was a pretty good trade, since I got it going with one whack of the red battery cable's clamp on the positive post. His kindness kept me off the road and on time to report to my duty station.

Fast forward to November: an ugly injury to my right leg and a month-long stay in Walter Reed. My ticket home after completing my school on crutches was for Thanksgiving Eve. I was unsure of both my physical and career prognosis; it depended on how well I mended following the long reconstruction to my leg. I wore an external, strapped-on immobilizer to position my knee in a 45-degree angle. One of my classmates heroically drove me down I-95 and to BWI airport in enough time to curb-check my bags and hobble to my gate.

I was just ahead of the standby hopefuls who would have preferred me to have missed their call to the precious seat going to Atlanta. Instead, I went on the plane ahead of the hatch closing. The only problem was I didn't fit in my ticketed middle seat. Not obliged to reassign seating, the flight attendant escorted me from the plane—accompanied by neither objections nor volunteers to switch seats for my benefit. I saw the happiness in the eyes of the standby fliers and wondered how to reorganize my trip home to Arkansas.

The government ticket on Eastern was rigid and limited in conversion ability; the counter agent rummaged through the computer to seek a way for me to get to Little Rock. Fortunately they had moved me and my visible problem to the end of their counter so their customers didn't have to witness the spectacle. The Delta counter agent did, and she asked to see my travel certificate. She asked me to relinquish it and wrote off twelve hundred dollars in fees to put me on Delta to Atlanta, where they were going to set me up with the rest of my itinerary. Dumbfounded and appreciative, I could only mutter "thank you" and go to the gate to wait for the flight.

You know how things work in air travel: the

best-laid plans, etc. My newfound ride toward home broke. We were deplaned because a cooling fan on the back of some dashboard gizmo failed. A replacement was to be flown up from Atlanta. What I didn't realize then was that my chances for a ride to Little Rock were flying away hour by hour.

I reached Atlanta at 2:00 a.m. and slept on benches. My clothes and toiletries had long since flown to Little Rock. My money for an afternoon flight ran out and I managed to line up a flight to Memphis on Thanksgiving Day. There I met my next night's lodging—more benches. I had spent my last money and only checked in with my folks by collect calls as I found out concrete details about my travels.

I don't recall the flight to Little Rock; I think I fell asleep on takeoff and woke to the flaring of the flaps on landing. My mom likes to describe the phalanx of uniformed airline employees who moved in an obvious team wedge up the hallway from the jetway, ahead of me by enough steps to be around one corner from me for almost the whole walk. She said they clearly knew of my experience by their actions and made it possible for me to move through the gate area with as much ease as I could muster.

The time from meeting my parents through the drive home to Hot Springs, Arkansas, is a blur to me, since I probably fell asleep. What I can relate is that in this period, well after Vietnam, there was no emotional, supportive outpouring for the uniformed service member. We did our work, served our time, or started careers. Some like me were rerouted in our lives without notice by our injuries. My college graduation plan was rendered worthless in less than a year.

I am exceedingly pleased to see recognition and outpouring toward service members in uniform in public places. I am happy to know that the public "sees" these citizens and often finds ways to thank them. It is well deserved, and it makes up in a small way for my own ridiculous experience.

Andrew
Pittsburgh, Pa.

When I took a position in Elizabethtown, Kentucky, near Fort Knox, I was invited by my recruiter to meet him with a couple of consultants. We met at a Chinese restaurant near the back gate of the post and went in for the buffet.

A group of six soldiers from the post were seated next to our table. My eyes fell on these young people and I recalled my years of service that went largely overlooked by the public as a whole. You see, I served between the wars in Vietnam and Kuwait. I have such pride in their service and the service of my two sons that I felt that I had to express it somehow. I talked to the guys that I was sitting with and convinced them to join me in buying the soldiers their lunches. We didn't stay to see how our little gift (about seven dollars apiece for them) was received, and wouldn't have felt comfortable doing so anyway.

I would like to thank you, Rose, for reminding all of us about the debt that we owe these fine young men and women.

Gary (Sgt. [Ret.], U.S. Army)

Rose, I told my son about your series on thanking soldiers. He has had a lot of problems from his two deployments to Iraq and is currently in the hospital. He was a gunner on top of various vehicles and he's had sixteen concussions during his two tours; he has received a Purple Heart. The Army is going to medically retire him due to severe brain trauma and the Posttraumatic Stress Disorder he suffers from, mostly due to his first tour in Fallujah. He asked me to spiffy up a note to you, as he has some problems with his organizational skills.

When he met the sergeant's board, he wasn't even able to do an about face (he turned the wrong direction), so that should give you an indication of where he's at. We are hoping that will get better with time. Here's his note.

Bonnie
Glenshaw, Pa. / Colorado Springs, Co.

Dear Rose,

My mom listens to you all the time and told me you are collecting stories about thanking soldiers. I am active-duty Army and can't get your program where I am stationed, but I wanted to share something with you.

I am married and have a daughter. My wife is young and I was in Iraq for fifteen months this last tour. My mom and dad both live in other states, so they are not able to come here as often as they like. Friends of my dad, Tucker and his wife, Nancy, looked after my wife and daughter the whole time I was gone. They checked in on them, took them to lunch, and gave my wife much-needed things for our daughter.

I returned home from my second tour in Iraq on Christmas Eve morning. I hadn't seen my daughter since she was three months old, so she had changed quite a bit. Something our friends did that really meant a lot was giving my wife a complete Christmas outfit for my daughter for her to wear on Christmas Day, when I would spend my first Christmas with her. It cost a bunch and she looked beautiful in her new little outfit.

It is really difficult for us to leave our loved ones for these long deployments. Having people like Tucker and Nancy donate their personal time, effort, and money to our loved ones who have been left behind means more than you can possibly imagine. Many of us have young spouses and small children who are on their own for at least a year. The kindness people show to our families helps us to feel more at ease—that someone is watching out for them when we can't be there.

Thank you for supporting us. We all appreciate it more than you know.

Scott (SPC 1, U.S. Army)

I am an officer in the U.S. Army Reserve. I have served for almost twenty years and have been deployed once to Iraq. I have recently been trying to make a decision about whether to retire or to stay and go through another deployment. I was leaning toward retirement when something happened that reminded me that I still have a duty to perform.

On a drill weekend, a group of us were leaving a restaurant after lunch. I was in front, and as I walked out the door I saw two elderly ladies helping a third, who was using a walker. I stood aside and held the outside door for them. As the lady with the walker got close to me, she reached out and grasped the sleeve of my uniform over my upper arm. She looked at me and said, "God bless you, soldiers." As I thanked her, I could see numbers tattooed on the inside of her arm.

I will think about her every time I need a reminder of why I should stay in the Army.

Andrew (U.S. Army Reserve)

Rose, I am a sergeant in the Pennsylvania Army National Guard. I listen to your show on a regular basis and appreciate your "Thanking a Soldier" segments. I live near your flagship city of Pittsburgh but my unit is located in the somewhat remote McKean County. For the last couple of years, some of my fellow soldiers and I have been playing golf at the local club when we get a few hours off in the evening. We always go in proper civilian attire but a few weeks ago I stopped in on my lunch break just to check on available tee times, and I was still in uniform.

That night, after we were released for the evening, we went to the course for nine holes of golf. Upon returning to the clubhouse to turn in our carts, the attendant asked me how many of us were soldiers. Not thinking much of it, I answered that there were four, and she quickly ran to the back room. She came back with four gift cards, each good for two free eighteen-hole rounds of golf. She handed them to me and simply said, "Thank you for your service." Naturally, I thanked her as well and passed out the gift cards to my fellow soldiers.

I would like to recognize the Kane Country Club in Kane, Pennsylvania, for its support of our troops. The club's gift was greatly appreciated.

Jon (Sgt., Pa. National Guard)

Hello again, Rose: I'm writing once more, not as a soldier that received a special "thanks" but as a witness to one.

Last night I was on my way to the hospital to meet my new nephew when I stopped at the local McDonald's for quick bite to eat. As I was pulling the door open, I could see someone in an Air Force uniform standing at the counter. Before I could think twice about it, a customer came up to the counter and told the clerk that she would like to pay for this airman's meal. I could tell the airman was taken aback and he asked why. The customer simply said, "Just because. Thank you for your service." The airman was very gracious and thanked the customer as she went back to her table.

I was truly moved by this act by a complete stranger. I don't know if this customer listens to your show, but I thought you should know that there are plenty of people out there who are so gracious to service members. I chatted with the airman briefly and found that he was in town shopping for a house. I hope that he, along with his wife and two children, do settle in my town—so that the next time I see him I can pick up his tab.

Jon

My Army National Guard unit in western Pennsylvania was in Iraq from March 2004 to March 2005. After completing this duty, we were still on active orders and had to work at the armory each day for a few weeks to unload, clean up, and put away equipment. One day at lunchtime, tired of eating the meals that the unit provided for us, several of my buddies and I went out to lunch at a local restaurant. It was the middle of the week and it wasn't crowded at lunchtime, although take-out and delivery seemed busy. There was only one other couple in the dining room. We were all just happy to be back and have a meal that wasn't an Army meal. As we were eating and telling our war stories, the other couple left without saying a word to us. When it was time to leave, we asked the waitress for our bill. She informed us that it had already been paid for by the other couple, who had left about five minutes earlier and who will remain forever anonymous.

David (Staff Sgt. [Ret.], U.S. Army)

I was stationed just south of Kuwait City with the Coast Guard Port Security Unit 308 (out of Gulfport, Mississippi). We had to go into Kuwait City for boat parts one day, so my friend and I tagged along just to get off the base. We actually went to the True Value store. A Kuwait City True Value is more like an American Sears and this one had a small cafe inside. My friend and I wanted a snack, so we ordered a pastry and cup of coffee. When we got up to pay, a Kuwaiti woman stopped us and, in broken English, asked us if we were in the Army. When we told her (from a distance) that we were in the U.S. Coast Guard, she would not let us pay for our meal! We thanked her and still tried to pay but she wouldn't let us, so we went back to the base.

One other short story is about my return to the States. As I was passing through Customs in Kentucky, the other passengers in line saw my camo and military bags and rushed me through to the front of the long line. As I left Customs on my way to my connection, a gentleman stopped me and asked me where I served. He also invited me into the Northwest Airlines Club under his membership (free food and drinks). I came home alone without my unit and missed the "official" welcome home, but was welcomed by my country.

Loren (U.S. Coast Guard)

I served in the U.S. Air Force from 1994 until 2002. In the fall of 2001 I was on a routine rotation to Bosnia when the tragic events of September 11 happened. I remained on site in Bosnia until early December 2001, when new replacements (and lots of extras) began to arrive (our typical rotation was only three months). My travel itinerary had me leaving Bosnia and flying back to Germany for outprocessing, and then to Denver through Chicago, as my home station was Peterson Air Force Base in Colorado Springs, Colorado.

I was accompanied on this trip by another member of my unit from Bosnia. As we boarded a large 737 aircraft to fly nonstop from Germany to Chicago, the flight attendant offered us an upgrade to first class. Looking around the plane we noticed that it was almost completely empty except for us, a

Muslim couple and their six children, and two other people who were already in first class. I looked back at the young couple with their children and then back to my partner, who gave me the approving nod. I then asked the flight attendant to offer that upgrade to the young family so that the kids could enjoy the fifteen-hour ride to Chicago.

The flight attendant went back to the couple and offered them the upgrade. Immediately the kids jumped up and sprinted to the first-class area, each of them high-fiving me as they went. The young woman then passed and hugged me. Knowing the traditions of that culture, I looked toward the husband, who answered the questions in my eyes by telling me that they were not as strict in their religion as some are, and that they were U.S. citizens who were trying to get back home to Cleveland, Ohio. We chatted for a few minutes and the young gentleman was impressed that I was not reacting like others who saw them board the plane. I explained that I had spent a lot of time overseas, including a two-year tour at Incirlik Air Base in Turkey, and that I knew there were a lot of people who perverted the religion. My travel partner and I spent the next fifteen hours listening to those children laugh and carry on up in first class; they also played a game of tag and hide and seek. It was one of the longest but most enjoyable and memorable flights I've ever had.

God had a special gift for me waiting at the

airport in Chicago. After collecting my luggage from baggage claim I was heading through the concourse to my connecting flight to Denver. (I should note here that prior to September 11 military members were discouraged from wearing their uniforms for travel; after September 11 we were required to wear them.) While walking toward the gate several people gave me encouraging nods and thumbs-up approvals. A little girl (about five years old) jumped off her seat, where she had been watching the ground crews load the planes, and sprinted right to me and stopped. Her mother, only a few steps behind, was trying to figure out what the little girl was doing; she called her name but the girl did not respond and just kept staring at me. I looked at her mother, who shrugged as if to say, "I don't know what she's doing." The girl then motioned with her finger for me to come closer, as if she had a secret to tell me. I knelt down on one knee, and without warning she threw her arms around me and whispered, "Thank you." My eyes filled with tears as I hugged her back and whispered, "You're welcome." It turns out that they were heading out to visit the girl's grandparents, and her grandfather, a Vietnam veteran, told her to say thank you to every soldier she met. I just happened to be the first one she saw.

I had never experienced such a day during my eight years in the Air Force. Second only to the births of my children, this remains one of my most precious memories and the reason I do all I can for those who have answered the call to service. I currently work for a large global-defense contractor whose motto is: "We Protect Those Who Protect Us." This allows me to continue to help our war fighters. This past Memorial Day I was privileged enough to be the coordinator of our golf outing, which we hosted in support of the Wounded Warrior Project. We were able to raise a thousand dollars.

George
Pittsburgh, Pa.

I am a soldier in the U.S. Army. This past Friday night I was going to a late dinner with my wife and as I was waiting for her I met a gentleman who noticed that I was in the military. When we finished dinner, the waitress said that our bill had been taken care of as a small thank-you for my service. I feel this gentleman was certainly one of your listeners.

Jim (CPD, U.S. Army Reserve)

I recently attended a showing of *Spiderman 3* here at LSA Anaconda (Balad Air Base, Iraq). We have a large auditorium that we use for movies as well as memorial services and other major gatherings. As is the custom back in the States, we stood and snapped to attention when the National Anthem began before the main feature. All was going as planned until about three-quarters of the way through the National Anthem the music stopped.

Now, what would happen if this occurred with a thousand eighteen-to-twenty-two-year-olds back in the States? I imagine there would be hoots, catcalls, laughter, a few rude comments, and everyone would sit down and yell for the movie to begin. Of course, that is, if they had stood for the National Anthem in the first place.

Here, the thousand soldiers continued to stand at attention, eyes fixed forward. The music started again. The soldiers continued to stand quietly at attention. And again, at the same point, the music stopped. What would you expect to happen? Even here I would imagine laughter as everyone sat down and anticipated the movie starting.

Here, you could have heard a pin drop. Every soldier stood at attention. Suddenly there was a lone voice, then a dozen, and quickly the room was filled with the voices of a thousand soldiers.

And the rockets' red glare,
the bombs bursting in air,
Gave proof through the night
that our flag was still there.

O say, does that star-spangled banner
yet wave
O'er the land of the free and the
home of the brave?

It was the most inspiring moment I have had here in Iraq. I wanted everyone to know what kinds of soldiers are serving their fellow citizens here.

Jim (Maj., Army National Guard; United Methodist pastor, Powder Springs, Ga.)

I work at a university Army ROTC and I have been an unwitting recipient of random acts of gratitude. Recently a coworker and I went to a local restaurant for lunch. Both of us were in uniform, and as we were finishing, the waiter told us, "The older gentleman that was sitting over there took care of your bill when he left and whenever you guys are done, you are good to go."

Another restaurant, Qdoba, in Pittsburgh, has always been a huge supporter of the military, and when there were protests at the nearby recruiting station, the restaurant offered free meals to any military personnel in uniform.

When I took over this job, my predecessor warned me that because there are very few military around I should be careful when walking in the city downtown while in uniform; but in recent months I have noticed just the opposite. I have gotten everything from random warm greetings to the Frito-Lay truck driver beeping his horn and giving me a thumbs-up and a big smile while driving by.

I don't deserve the recognition—I'm just doing my job—but I appreciate that people are supportive. At a strategic level, I hope this goodwill and support bleeds over into a willingness to let us finish the job in the Middle East and listen to the senior military leaders. Before I returned from Iraq last June, General Petraeus came down for a ceremony where he placed combat patches on our soldiers. I have met him many times, and I was proud to serve under such an astute and competent leader.

Daniel (Maj., U.S. Army)

As an American soldier, it is my distinct privilege to serve this great country, and I have been proudly serving since May 1998. I was chosen to command a recruiting company (both active duty and Reserve component) in western Pennsylvania several years ago.

During these years there have been numerous occasions when people have thanked me for my service. One particular day was the most memorable. I was eating breakfast with my first sergeant, my husband, and a good friend on the morning of my promotion to major. When we were finished, we learned that someone had paid for our breakfast. It was a very touching experience. As this was a momentous day in my career, I was getting ready to make the transition to field-grade officer and I felt an overwhelming sense of appreciation.

I have attempted to do the same in return for other service members since that time. While my husband has been attending school at Fort Benning, Georgia, I have traveled frequently to and from Atlanta. The Atlanta airport is always filled with soldiers returning and departing to and from Iraq and Afghanistan. I make it a point to thank each of them for their service and to buy them lunch as a small token of appreciation.

Danielle (Maj., U. S. Army, MI, Commanding)

I am a former Army captain who separated from service several years ago. When I left the military I went to work for a startup company in Georgia. The company was already in bad financial shape when I was hired, but it took about six months before it became very obvious we were in trouble.

I decided to forego pay for half a year in an attempt to give us the funding needed to complete our product development before I made the decision to move on.

I live near an Army airfield that has a special-operations aviation unit, which was preparing to deploy about the time I was struggling with the decision to move on.

I was in a restaurant having a cup of coffee and a soldier from the unit was eating his breakfast about three seats away. At that moment it hit me like a ton of bricks: My problems, in the big scheme of things, were really small compared to what that young specialist was about to do for the next year or so of his life.

I had lived off my savings and investments during this period and was getting close to my final thousand dollars in cash reserves, but I paid for my coffee with a twenty-dollar bill and told the waitress that the soldier's money was no good.

I had faith that whatever was troubling me would go away within a year and I also knew from experience that some of those soldiers wouldn't make it through a year. So, the gratefulness I felt in making this one soldier's morning a little better helped me put my problems in perspective.

Gregg (Capt. [Ret.], U.S. Army)

I am the commander for an army recruiting station in western Pennsylvania. As a proud member of our Armed Forces and one of three members of the United States Army in my family, I have had several acts of kindness from complete strangers while out eating or frequenting other places of business in the area. Army recruiters deal with much negativity, so when we have someone show appreciation for what we do it makes a big difference to us. I greatly appreciate the support we receive, and I especially want to thank you, Rose, and the radio show for standing up for what we believe in and what we as members of the Armed Forces defend on a daily basis.

William (Staff Sgt., U.S. Army, Station Commander)

Rose, here is my story as close as I can remember from six decades ago.

Korea, 1950: I was seventeen years old at the time and made the first combat jump with the 187th Airborne Regimental Combat Team at Sunchon, North Korea. That's when General MacArthur said the war would be over by Christmas, until the Chinese army came into the mix.

On our way south we kept the main supply

route open, walking most of the way. In those high mountain passes, at nearly 60 degrees below zero, our weapons had a hard time functioning.

Second combat jump was at Munsan-ni in the spring of 1951.

It is so nice now to see our returning fighting men getting recognized for the things they are doing for our great country. It wasn't like that when I returned home from Korea. When rotating combat personnel landed in Seattle (I think), there were no people to greet us. The returning soldiers always need to feel the gratitude from their fellow Americans.

Thanks for telling people to help the veterans in any way they can.

David (Korean War veteran)
Charleroi, Pa.

5
Helping Hands: Organizations and Websites

Everyone working at my dental office is very patriotic and tries to do his or her part each day. My wife sends care packages on a monthly basis to my patients who are serving in the military. We have sent many dental-supply kits to Iraq through the **Yellow Ribbon Girls,** a support group from Ellwood City, Pennsylvania (**www.yellowribbongirls.com**). We decorate a bulletin board in the waiting room to welcome home those who serve. We pick up the tab for military personnel when we see them eating out. But what really touched me, and the reason I am writing, was what happened last Monday.

One young soldier who returned home recently came in for some dental work; he had no coverage, so I treated him for free. That is not why I am writing this to you. I am writing to let you know that the girls who work for me told me that they did not want to be paid either and insisted that I deduct their payroll for the hour that we treated this young soldier.

I know that my staff is the best in the world and I am very lucky to have them, but what they did on Monday made me so proud that I just had to share it with you. There really are good people out there.

Joseph
Beaver Falls, Pa.

For those people who can't hang out near army bases and airports, **Adopt a Platoon** (**www.adopta-platoon.org**) is a great way to help. It's a very personal way to make a contribution. I have received e-mails from my soldiers and feel extremely honored that they would take the time and effort to thank me. To be even a tiny part of raising the morale of our troops makes me feel like I'm part of the fight.

I have another story to share. I was in my local video store, buying DVDs for one of my soldiers. When I told the manager what I was doing, she thought it was a wonderful idea, being the mother of a recently returned soldier. She got the idea of having a collection box where patrons can donate DVDs. That was about a year ago and they still have the box in the front of the store.

Leslie
Scottdale, Pa.

Two weeks ago, I e-mailed **www. auntnancyusa.com (Aunt Nancy USA: Support the Troops)** to get the name of a soldier that we could "adopt." She e-mailed me back with the name and military address of a soldier by the name of Joshua, but she had no other information about him. My nine-year-old daughter, seven-year-old son, and I immediately started packing a goody box for Joshua and getting it into the mail so that he would have it by Christmas. We included a lot of small items from the list that Aunt Nancy suggested and also a personal letter from us, with pictures of our kids and drawings that the kids had made for "our" soldier.

This afternoon, UPS delivered a box addressed to my son and daughter. I assumed it had been ordered by my husband from work and contained Christmas presents—but when he came home, my husband claimed that he had ordered nothing to be sent directly to the kids. We took the box upstairs and opened it, to find it loaded with all kinds of beautiful art supplies and wooden picture frames. The name of the shipper on the packing slip was none other than our soldier, Joshua.

I can tell you that it was quite a few minutes before either my husband or I could speak. We had so wanted to brighten the Christmas for one lonely soldier, and he had in turn blessed us with this thoughtful and generous gift. Our military personnel are truly the salt of the earth, and we are most fortunate to have them. Please ask your listeners again to pray daily for these wonderful soldiers. It's the very least we can do—we all owe them so much.

Jill
Steubenville, Ohio

I moved from Ohio to North Carolina four years ago. In December at my new office, the girls were talking about a Secret Santa gift exchange. They wanted to spend five dollars each on everyone in the office. Instead, I suggested we pool the funds and send the money to **Treats for Troops** (**www.treatsfortroops.info**). We've done it every year since! The people at Treats for Troops are wonderful. You tell them what you want to spend and if you have any preferences on what you want to buy—or, they will do it all for you! Sure beats Christmas shopping for a dozen five-buck trinkets!

Charlita
Rockingham, N.C.

Because of Sunday morning activities, I rarely get to see any of *Fox News Sunday*. It just so happens that on October 2, I caught the end of the broadcast, and they were highlighting their Power Player of the Week. It was Hal at Fran O'Brien's Steakhouse, who had been putting on Friday night dinners for severely wounded troops and their families from Walter Reed. I had been thinking about how to show support, and I decided this was a good way. I contacted Hal, and my family sponsored our first dinner the following March. Since then, we have sponsored and attended three more dinners, with another one scheduled in February.

You can do the math: A good steak dinner and drinks for seventy-five to a hundred people is not cheap, but this is the best investment we have ever made. We have been treated with such gratitude and kindness from military people in the Washington, D.C., area. We have met some incredible people.

Meeting these heroic soldiers is a wonderful experience, and when they thank us for buying them dinner, it's all I can do to keep from breaking down. The honor is all ours. I tell people that are ambivalent about the war to take a little time from their distraught lives and visit some or all of the places we go to as often as possible: Ground Zero … The Flight 93 Crash and Memorial site … Arlington National

Cemetery ... The Marine Corps Museum. If visiting these places does not stir you, you are either not an American or you are not living.

Let everyone know that they can donate to the **Aleethia Foundation**—the organization that does all of this and more (**www.aleethia.org**).

Just a quick update. We did not sponsor a dinner in February, but we did sponsor one last Friday at the Capitol Hill Club in D.C. After spending some time at Arlington, we enjoyed dinner with about seventy-five people—severely wounded troops, their families, the Aleethia supporters, and other military personnel. We met the outgoing and incoming military advisors to the Undersecretary of Defense—two generals who told me that if I ever needed anything to just give them a call. I had triple amputees thanking me for dinner. All I can say is that it was an honor to help in any way.

Brian
Penn Township, Pa.

Requests for bibles for our troops continue to pour in. A recent note received:

"My husband's cousin is in charge of a brigade in Iraq and we would like to send bibles to his whole brigade. They have already lost a sergeant. We could probably find out where to send them. How much would this cost? I believe there are seven hundred men and women in all. We have been praying for a way to reach these soldiers. Thank you."

Since the beginning of this year, **Campus Crusade for Christ's Military Ministry (www.militaryministry.org)** has been receiving requests for an average of close to twenty thousand Rapid Deployment Kits per month with free bibles.

Megan
Director, Donor Relations
Campus Crusade for Christ, International

Several years ago our veterans group, mostly comprised of Vietnam vets, decided to let some active military personnel know their service was appreciated. During that time things globally were relatively quiet and peaceful. Some of the Post members had family serving in the military. We sent six boxes of candy—costing five dollars each—to six different soldiers serving within the United States. The cost of the candy and postage was approximately fifty dollars, and that was a lot of money for us at that time.

The responses we received from those little tokens of appreciation were overwhelming. So we decided to gather names and addresses of military personnel and send cards, letters, and a few comfort items on a more regular basis. By mid-2001 we were sending monthly packages to thirty soldiers!

Then 9/11 happened. It wasn't long and things picked up immensely. In December 2002 we were sending to over two hundred soldiers all around the world—to Japan, Italy, Korea, Iceland, Spain, Germany, and other countries. We watched with the world as the troops moved across the desert into Baghdad. At that time, our soldiers arrived before many of their supplies. Soldiers' needs were conveyed to us through family members—they need toilet paper and female products. One female soldier told us, "You won't believe what we're using for feminine hygiene products!" So the boxes were shipped as quickly as we could gather donations.

Today, they are more comfortable on their bases than they were a few short years ago. Our packages continue to be sent on a monthly basis. Approximately seventy-five boxes are shipped each month, except for December. We ship about ten times that amount at Christmastime so everyone can have a nice holiday.

The Vietnam War taught us an invaluable lesson—no matter your opinion of the war, it is critical to support the soldiers. We are totally committed to doing that, whether it is in wartime or peacetime.

No soldier's service should be forgotten or taken for granted.

Laurie
Project Support Our Troops
A project of the Veterans' Welcome Home Association
(*www.post52.com/index.php?pr=Project_Support_Our_Troops*)

Just passing on another great site for helping the troops. This lady, Jeanette (from Hilton Head Island, South Carolina), bakes cookies for the troops and sends them to the Middle East through an organization called **Treat the Troops (www.treatthetroops.org)**.

Herb
Mercer, Pa.

Rose, I am hoping that you can help me get the word out about another organization doing great work on behalf of severely wounded veterans. The group is called **Homes for Our Troops,** and its website is

www.homesforourtroops.org. One of the houses they are building is in Ross Township in the Pittsburgh area. Their motto is: "Building Specially Adapted Homes for Our Severely Injured Veterans, at No Cost to the Veterans We Serve."

Dan
Cranberry Township, Pa.

Rose, I wanted to encourage your listeners that one of the greatest gifts that they could give a military family (or any grieving family, for that matter) is a memory letter.

A second gift idea would be that they can pay the membership fee for the surviving spouse/parent to enroll in either the **Gold Star Wives of America** and/or **Gold Star Mothers** groups.

Gold Star Wives (**www.goldstarwives.org**) and Gold Star Mothers (**www.goldstarmoms.com**) are organizations that fight for the military benefits that families receive after the death of their loved one. They can also be of great support emotionally as well when you meet other members either in person or online in a chat group.

I did not learn about these groups from my casualty assistance officer assigned to me by the military, but instead by another aviation widow whom I met after my husband's death.

Stephanie
Steubenville, Ohio

I am hoping to get the word out about a great organization for the troops: **Soldiers' Angels.**

Want to help but don't know how? Want to send a thank-you to a soldier? Or send treats to the Military Working Dogs? You can adopt a hero to send packages to or join one of our many specialized teams, from letter writing to sewing and baking angels!

Join **Soldiers' Angels** at **www.soldiersangels.org** and be an angel to the soldiers who give so unselfishly for us!

If you check us out at www.soldiersangels.org you will see that we are a great organization and we reach out to so many of our troops—and they desperately need us.

Trish
Peters Township, Pa.

Other Organizations and Websites for Extending a Hand to Our Deserving Military Members

The author/publisher does not specifically endorse, nor assure the legitimacy of, nor guarantee positive experiences with, any of the organizations listed in this chapter. In addition, many other groups are certainly worthy of attention. Readers are encouraged to research each of these organizations to their own satisfaction.

Air Force Aid Society:
www.afas.org

American Freedom Foundation:
www.americanfreedomfoundation.org

Army Emergency Relief:
www.aerhq.org

Blue Star Mothers of America:
www.bluestarmothers.org

Coast Guard Mutual Assistance:
www.cgmahq.org

Fisher House Foundation:
www.fisherhouse.org

Freedom Alliance:
www.freedomalliance.org

Give2theTroops:
www.give2thetroops.org

Keep the Faith Foundation:
www.keepthefaithfoundation.org

Let's Say Thanks:
www.letssaythanks.com

LOOC Foundation:
(Kelsey Grammer Leadership Fellows):
www.looc.org

Military Families United:
www.militaryfamiliesunited.org

National Remember Our Troops Campaign:
www.nrotc.org

Navy-Marine Corps Relief Society:
www.nmcrs.org

Operation Homefront:
www.operationhomefront.net

Operation Mom:
www.operationmom.org

Operation Payback:
www.operationpayback.ning.com

Operation Shoebox:
www.operationshoebox.com

Operation Soldier Assist:
www.soldierassist.com

Operation Troop Aid:
www.operationtroopaid.org

Operation Troop Appreciation:
www.operationtroopappreciation.org

Operation Care and Comfort:
www.occ-usa.org

Special Operations Warrior Foundation:
www.specialops.org

Tea Party Vets:
www.teapartyvets.org

The Gratitude Campaign:
www.gratitudecampaign.org

Troops Need You:
www.troopsneedyou.com

United Service Organizations:
(USO): www.uso.org

Veterans Outreach Center:
www.veteransoutreachcenter.org

Warriors Watch:
www.warriorswatch.org

Wounded Warrior Project:
www.woundedwarriorproject.com

*A special thanks to our radio audience.
If it were not for their generosity
there would not be a book.*

—Rose